Why Should You Read This Book?

Many people are waiting for *Normal* to return. They ask questions like:

> ➤ Shouldn't the economy, and hiring, return to *Normal* soon?
> ➤ Won't the government continue as *Normal*?
> ➤ When can I recover my losses and achieve a *Normal* rate of return in my retirement account?

But *Normal* doesn't live here anymore. In *Normal's* place, three newcomers—*Uncertainty, Complexity, and Constant Change*—have moved in. The new economy has arrived.

Past assumptions of economic and political order no longer apply, and the key to success lies in having your Plan B ready when Plan A doesn't work anymore. This book will help you prepare your Plan B by providing you with:

> ➤ Authoritative predictions,
> ➤ Down-to-earth strategies,
> ➤ Documented facts and analysis,
> ➤ And, importantly, first hand, real-world experience.

**You want to win in the new economy.
Read on and find out how.**

WHAT'S YOUR PLAN B?

WHAT'S YOUR PLAN B?

WIN IN THE NEW ECONOMY

L.A. Jenkins

Two Harbors Press
212 3rd Avenue North, Suite 290
Minneapolis, MN 55401
612.455.2293
www.TwoHarborsPress.com

ISBN-13: 978-1-936401-28-4
LCCN: 2011923730

Distributed by Itasca Books

Printed in the United States of America

To my late wife, Cyndee,
who inspired me to start this book. . .

. . . and to my dear Mary,
who encouraged me to finish it.

Contents

PART THREE: HOW TO WIN IN THE NEW ECONOMY

Preface

The Industrial Age economy no longer dominates the Western world, and we now find ourselves in a new multi-faceted global economy imposing a high degree of complexity, uncertainty, and change upon our lives. Simplicity has been displaced by complex systems, overflowing with options subject to a wide range of restrictions and potential threats. Uncertainty as to what may come next has replaced stability and predictability. Nothing seems to stand still, even for a moment. Change is constant.

This book focuses on America's transition to a post-Industrial Age, referred to as the Global Innovation Age, for which the nation is largely unprepared. For those people and organizations that are not ready, this new age holds the prospect of a bleak future. However, a world of opportunity awaits the creative and aggressive.

The goal of *What's Your Plan B?* is not to depress or frighten you, though this book will undoubtedly conjure up some of those emotions. The objectives are to portray the marketplace challenges that await you and help you to develop your own plan of action to win in the new economy. The information in this book will help you and your organization find the route to success in the Global Innovation Age.

Plenty of experts and leaders state, with solemn certainty, their visions of the future and what should be done. *What's Your Plan B?* doesn't claim the future is absolute. All that can be done is: assess the situation at a particular point in time, form a series of scenarios that are likely outcomes, and then assign probabilities to each scenario. Finally, it is necessary to establish benchmarks and monitor events as they unfold to ensure that the assumptions underlying the original projected scenarios are still valid.

A willingness to change one's plans when presented with new facts is a requirement if you are to succeed in the new economy. However, this statement infers a degree of adaptability that many people and organizations are unable or unwilling to accept. Such adaptability will be one of your most powerful tools to win in the new economy.

Forecasting the future is not a precise science. Trends and predictions can provide a general direction for moving ahead, but specific results and details will vary. In addition, underlying assumptions can be changed by events, so the importance of attaching probabilities to predictions can't be overstated. Moreover, as future events take place, probabilities for any given prediction will change.

Why not just wait to see what happens and then react accordingly? A key to winning is to know what *not* to do as much as what to do. In particular, a winner avoids doing the wrong thing in the wrong place at the wrong time. Once an event takes place, it will likely be too late to do the right thing, unless prior planning and preparation has taken place.

In short, the route across the "big unknown" ahead isn't a well-marked highway. The process for moving ahead is more like following the general direction of a compass and reading markers along the way to jump from path to path. This book can assist you with planning and preparing for the journey, but you have to be willing and able to do what is necessary for successfully arriving at your destination.

How to Gain the Most Out of This Book

Don't skip the first part, "What in the World Is Going On?" This part provides an overview of the changes and conflicts facing post-Industrial Age America. Answer the questions at the end of the chapter "The War for Control of the Future" to the extent that you, your organization, and your government officials have moved beyond Industrial Age thinking.

The next part, "10 Trends You Can't Ignore," discusses important trends affecting your life, business, career, and retirement. There are other trends, but these should be among your top priorities. Numerous foreign sources were accessed and cited in researching these trends to provide a global perspective.

Each trend contains predictions, along with the applicable probabilities. A 50 percent probability indicates that consideration of alternative scenarios is warranted; a probability of 65 percent or higher is something to bet on rather than against; and a probability of 80 percent or over is something not to be ignored. For an updated probability of each prediction, go to **www.jenkinsusa.com**. These predictions and probabilities were prepared between January and May, 2010, and projected to occur within the next ten years, unless stated otherwise. In addition, each trend discussion concludes with winning strategies for us, as a nation; winning strategies for you, as a leader; and winning strategies for you, personally, as suggestions to win in the new economy.

The third part, "How to Win in the New Economy," focuses on helping you develop your own plan of action to survive and succeed during this time of upheaval. You'll learn ways to protect the value of your money and stay right side up in upside-down markets. Just as importantly, you will gain insight on how to turn uncertainty, complexity, and constant change into opportunity. Finally, in an age where billions of dollars seem like pocket change, be sure to read the appendix, "How Much Is a Trillion Dollars?" for a reality check.

You can't drive into the future by staring in the rearview mirror!
Turn the page and take a clear look at the road ahead.

PART ONE:
WHAT IN THE WORLD
IS GOING ON?

The War for Control of the Future

It Wasn't Supposed to Be This Way

Prepare yourself, America. You're about to go to war . . .

But before you roll out the high-tech weaponry and lace up those combat boots, hold on. This is not going to be a conventional war. In fact, this war will be a series of battles unlike any we've ever fought before. For the most part, the weapons of choice will be ideas, information, and networks, but rest assured there will be pain and suffering—and casualties as well. The conflict will be global, but it will also reach into our factories, shops, and classrooms. When bloodshed occurs, it will often be conducted in ways for which we are unprepared.

In the Industrial Age, the future was expected to march seamlessly on to innovations that would make our lives better and our work more fulfilling. We could

Are You Prepared?
The transition to a post-Industrial Global Innovation Age will be tumultuous, with potentially catastrophic consequences for those unprepared to deal with it and the accompanying uncertainty, complexity, and constant change.

hope to live to 100, increase our leisure time, and provide an even more interesting and comfortable lifestyle. A new Global Innovation Age promised new opportunities, replacing the gritty industrial character of America. However, the change-over from the Industrial Age economy to a new globalized economy isn't going to be as smooth and predictable as we once hoped.

The transition to a post-Industrial Global Innovation Age will be tumultuous, with potentially catastrophic consequences for the people and organizations unprepared to deal with it. Profound political, social, and economic structural changes will cause extraordinary upheaval and conflict. Long sacrosanct assumptions in America—such as each succeeding generation expecting to enjoy a more affluent life than the one before—are no longer a "sure thing."

The tumult is more than simply the conflict between liberals and conservatives or debates between Republicans and Democrats. The solution is not simply a matter of injecting a bit more capitalism or socialism into the drowning economy. Much more is at stake. America is at a critical point of redefining itself.

The transition to a post-industrial society is a major turning point in our history, similar in some respects to the period leading up to and including America's Civil War. At that time, the Northern states comprised a nascent industrial economy. Contrarily, the Southern states were determined to preserve an agrarian-based status quo. The social, political, and economic conflicts eventually escalated to war. In this sense, the Civil War was an example of the fading Agriculture Age turned upside down by the overwhelming force of the Industrial Age.

> **Global Convergence**
> The Age of Global Innovation will lead to Global Convergence. Living standards will rise in emerging market nations, offset by declining or stagnant living standards in industrialized economies that can't adapt to global innovation.

Now, the post-Industrial Global Innovation Age is challenging the last vestiges of America's Industrial Age. Assembly lines are shut down, factories shuttered, and their workers pink-slipped, but the Industrial Age infrastructure of institutions, vested interests, and power elites (and those dependent upon them) continue to exist. Some adapt, while others seek restrictions on trade and innovation to preserve their status quo or expand their influence. They will not give up power without a fight. However, in a global economy empowered by the Internet, digital technology, and intellectual capital, the fading forces of the Industrial Age are succumbing to the overwhelming power of the Global Innovation Age.

The world, as we've known it, will be upended and societal tensions aggravated as the post-Industrial Age progresses. Consider the following:

> ➢ **Global innovation will produce dramatic shifts in prices**, along with growing access to goods, services, and—perhaps most importantly—ideas from around the world. The effect will be two-fold. First, consumers will enjoy access to more affordable products and services. Second, inevitably, the number of consumers around the world will grow, dramatically increasing new market opportunities. So, what's the problem with this scenario? Those industries and government services that can't adapt will disappear, right? Well, they should, but a multitude of obsolete business models will be kept alive through trade protectionism, subsidy, and bailout programs as governments desperately engage in acts of political expediency to "save" jobs. One result of such policies is to make products and services less affordable or not accessible at all. Another result is to limit global opportunities as other nations retaliate against U.S. protectionism. In the longer run, protectionism only causes the "saved" jobs to become less secure and less reward-

ing, meanwhile reducing the creation of new jobs. And what is the result? A frustrated and angry workforce.

➢ **Innovation processes will become extremely well developed and invigorated** by literally *tens of millions* of scientists, entrepreneurs, and inventors (on a global scale) within a decade. Consequently, innovations will become increasingly inexpensive and quick to implement—and duplicate. Besides obsolescing slow-moving industries with quick dispatch, government review and permit bodies will become less relevant. Consumers, empowered by the Internet and other technologies, will know "If I can't buy it here, I can buy it elsewhere," with the potential for circumventing government controls and regulations. In turn, governments will likely try to limit individual access to sources outside the country.

➢ **The Global Innovation Age will lead to Global Convergence** over the next ten to twenty years. Wealth and power will become more dispersed around the world. Living standards will rise in emerging market nations and be offset by declining or stagnant living standards in industrialized economies that don't adapt to the impact of global innovation.

The Battle Lines Form

The war for control of the future (*your* future) is being waged on various fronts. Expect the battles to be costly, painful, and to last a very long time. On one front are the Defenders of the Industrial Age in the media, government, labor, and business sectors, those who call for the "re-industrialization" of America. They make no secret of their desire for America to return to "the good old days" of the Industrial Age. They favor imposing tariffs and other restrictions on foreign trade, thus creating an insular, controlled economy that will allegedly "manage" the impact of globalism to avoid serious threats to their power and position.

The Defenders of the Industrial Age are joined by the power elites of Big Government, Big Labor, and the remnants of Big Industry (as epitomized by GM prior to its bankruptcy). Their survival is dependent on Industrial Age thinking. They claim they understand the impact of globalism and technology and call for America to move forward in the pursuit of change—without sacrifice to their special interest groups and in a manner that maintains or increases their power.

The Guardians of the Status Quo can be found almost anywhere. These are the people (and organizations) who favor incremental change versus game-changing innovation. Their money, power, and egos are dependent on stable, predictable environments. While they do openly acknowledge the passing of the Industrial Age (and are often tech-savvy themselves), they are resistant to major change and susceptible to the arguments of the Defenders of the Industrial Age.

The most dangerous of the Guardians of the Status Quo are the thug-like bosses heading nations like Venezuela and Iran. The leading commodity produced in these countries is oil, the Industrial Age's "black gold." At some point, the dissent in their countries will become so great from the misery inflicted on the population that a distraction will be necessary. War serves that purpose. After all, these leaders stand to be toppled if they do nothing, so the risk of war becomes a calculated bet to stay in power.

Intellectual capital is becoming the real wealth of nations, organizations, and individuals rather than plants, equipment, and inventory. While the Defenders of the Industrial Age have squandered the wealth generated during their reign, a new set of contenders has arrived on the world stage by nurturing their intellectual capital as a powerful resource.

These contenders, the Innovators, won't simply disappear or allow the wealth they produce to be confiscated. They'll move themselves or their ideas to other places on the globe where better opportunities beckon. Digital technology affords the Innovators the ability to work anywhere and confront the Defenders of the Industrial Age and their allies. Focusing on intellectual firepower, game-changing innovation, customer-centric strategies, operational flexibility, and global networks, the Innovators will gain the upper hand over time. However, punitive legislation, litigation, and taxation are powerful weapons in the hands of the Innovators' enemies.

Globalism extends beyond business. Entertainment and the arts are blossoming in emerging nations as their populations grow more affluent. Innovative elected officials in the public sector are challenging the status quo of governance with radical ideas to reinvent their communities.

In the Industrial Age, wars were won by attrition. That is, the side that could out-produce the enemy in terms of troops, steel, and oil possessed the upper hand. In the Global Innovation Age, however, superior intellectual firepower and digital capabilities will provide the advantage.

Finally, the third front of the battle also requires attention. Islamic terrorists opposed to both sides are trying to impose a medieval theocracy on the world. They don't do battle via courts or competition; they cut off heads and blow up children. They are not bound by the rules of political correctness that American troops must follow. They turn our technology against us. The most outlandish science fiction could not provide a stranger, more difficult enemy to conquer.

Avoiding the Crossfire

For you, the big question is: "How do we capitalize on the vast opportunities of the Global Innovation Age and the resulting new economy without becoming a casualty of the inevitable conflicts?" The starting point is to define the problem. The end of the industrial state, as we've come to know it, isn't the primary issue. Rather, the real issue stems from millions of American workers and businesses—along with the government and major institutions—that are simply unprepared for the changes brought about by the emergence of the post-industrial state.

A shake-up that only rearranges the boxes in the organizational charts of the status quo won't be enough to compete effectively in the Global Innovation Age. You and your organization must act, and act quickly, to move ahead and avoid being trapped in the crossfire of the forces battling for control of the future.

Prelude to a Different Kind of War

The evolutionary pattern of the post-Industrial Age is fodder for endless debate and analysis. Terminology and a historical perspective of dates are subject to differing opinions. However, to provide a simplified context for understanding the issues presented in this book, the following history will hopefully prove helpful.

The 1980s

A confluence of technological, economic, social, and political movements washed up and over the bulwarks of the Industrial Age during the decade of the 1980s. Some observers refer to this period as "The Information Age." It was a time in which Industrial Age institutions, culture, and premises were challenged. As they made their way into the marketplace, new technologies such as personal computers, voicemail recorders, and fax machines reflected a fresh burst of innovative change. The digital revolution kicked into high gear. Barriers to entry for businesses dropped as information and access to capital became increasingly available. Database development and access diminished the power of the locked file cabinet as critical information was disseminated among a larger population.

Lower tax rates, economic expansion, and relaxed regulation brought forth corporate raiders and new competitors, forcing large corporations to retrench their organizations and focus on shareholder value. Big Government was still stomping around, but it was reined in by President Ronald Reagan's conservative policies. Reagan's firing of striking air traffic controllers in 1981 reflected an ongoing shift in the fortunes of Big Labor. Union membership in the private sector, after reaching its zenith in 1978 with about 20.5 million workers, was in a long downward trend.

Entrepreneurship and the "yuppie" (young urban professional) phenomenon were emblematic of a new era of risk-taking and the decline of the traditional paternalistic practices of large corporations. Silicon Valley symbolized innovation and capitalism in America. Michael J. Fox's portrayal of Alex P. Keaton on the NBC sitcom *Family Ties* epitomized the new social, economic, and political paradigm.

Big industry was forced to downsize, right size, and reinvent itself to survive. The demise of the typewriter during this period is symbolic of the Industrial Age, an iconic and ubiquitous tool that faded away to obsolescence. But this was just the first wave to reach the shore leading to modern globalism.

The 1990s

The take-off of the Internet could be likened to injecting the era of digital technology with steroids. Enhanced online and other information capabilities enabled the Age of Global Innovation to coalesce. Traditional distribution and cost structures collapsed, timeframes shrank, and the capability to move products, services, and money around the globe was transformed.

The advent of the Internet marked the breach of all the remaining storm control measures put in place by the Industrial Age institutions.

Big Government acted with restraint under the administration of centrist President Bill Clinton, whose mantra was, "It's the economy, stupid." Federal deficits were tamed, international trade agreements were expanded, and a welfare reform plan was implemented, actually producing some of the desired results. Against this backdrop, a huge tax increase was absorbed, and the U.S. dollar was strengthened against other currencies.

Big Labor made up some of its membership losses via the public sector as growing tax revenues and financial markets, swollen with investment funds, gobbled up government debt and made it easy for politicians to say "Yes" to unionized public employees.

Big Business experienced a resurgence during the Clinton administration as well. Having slimmed down the prior decade, businesses learned to use the new technologies to "do more with less."

The New Millennium (the 00s)

In the first decade of the new millennium, it was apparent that the Industrial Age in the U.S. was on its way out. The manufacturing base of the U.S. was being hollowed out as factories moved to China and other countries. Outsourcing of call centers and other services to foreign countries with lower labor costs became viable, thanks to global telecom grids.

Much of the U.S. steel industry (Big Steel) folded into a series of bankruptcy proceedings, despite protectionist tariffs invoked by a Big Government president (George Bush "43") to keep steel prices up. However, higher prices weren't the panacea for the steel companies' fatal downward spiral. Archaic business models and aggressive global competitors flush with cash from supplying the fast-growing BRIC (Brazil, Russia, India, and China) economies thrust the final blow.

September 11, 2001, marked a cataclysmic historical event. This was not an Industrial Age type of action; rather, it was a new form of high-tech and counter-tech war waged by extra-national terrorists extolling a medieval-like culture. Suddenly, what should have been the plot for an apocalyptic science fiction movie became all too much of a reality as the world watched in shock and horror.

The Bush administration turned on the money spigots and blessed the Greenspan Federal Reserve Bank in flooding the nation with cheap and easy money to refloat the economy after 9/11. Asset inflation took place and debt levels climbed because borrowing costs were artificially cheap, thanks to the Fed.

The dot.coms rebuilt the Internet industry on new business model applications that weaved the web into the fabric of our lives and work. The economy rose along with the tide of easy money flooding the economy, all courtesy of the Fed. A hot topic was an anticipated shortage of workers as the Baby Boomers took early retirement, thus spawning a new generation of affluent retirees who would spend freely and keep the economy percolating along.

The Blackberry and the iPhone could serve as popular technological visual markers for the first decade of the new millennium. Information, entertainment, and communication became mobile and nearly instantaneous, going with the user rather than the user going to the source. Being "connected" morphed from "plugged in" to "online all the time."

The 2010s

Many people have attributed the economic recession—which officially began in December 2007—to the subprime loan crisis. However, as is usually the case, there is more to it than that.

Essentially, the U.S. government has been and continues to prop up a system still primarily premised and structured on the model of an industrial state. Consumers, businesses, and investors have been encouraged to leverage to the hilt on the assumption of a reasonably predictable future based on Industrial Age expectations.

In short, at the time of this writing, the U.S. continues to live beyond its means for political expediency rather than investing in infrastructure and preparing its population to support life in the new Global Innovation Age. America's high-tech, globally competitive resources are trapped inside the decrepit body of Industrial Age legal, political, and social institutions. In many ways, America is on the verge of becoming a subprime economy, living beyond its means and paying for its excesses by incurring debt it cannot plausibly pay back based on its current circumstances.

But the story doesn't stop here, even amidst a heap of doom and gloom. As you read this, innovative Americans are devising ways of circumventing the remnants of the Industrial Age that are blocking their way. Trends do not extend into perpetuity, and their direction *can* be changed. We have a choice to make. Will we allow ourselves to be handcuffed to Industrial Age thinking and watch our futures whither away, or will we make the structural changes necessary for America to assume leadership of the Global Innovation Age?

The Global Innovation Age vs. the Industrial Age

Are you still a little murky on the Industrial Age versus the Age of Global Innovation? On the following page are a few additional signs (or symptoms) of each condition. Where do you fit? Where does your organization fit?

Industrial Age Thinking	Global Innovation Age Realities
Old media, newspapers	Digital-based information technologies
Libraries of encyclopedias	Online all the time
Landline telephones	Mobile technology
Union manufacturing plants	Outsourcing
Traditional hub-and-spoke airlines	Anywhere, anytime global flexibility
Mass production	Mass customization
Office buildings to house staff	Telecommuting
Face-to-face meetings	Phone/videoconferencing
Traditional public school curriculums	Individualized world-class education
Cards and letters	Facebook and texting
Paternalistic policies	You're on your own, baby

PART TWO:
10 TRENDS
YOU CAN'T IGNORE

Trend 1

The Contingency Plan *IS* the Plan

Preparing for the Unpredictable and the Utterly Unimaginable

"Nobody saw this coming!"
"It was unpredictable!"
"I didn't think it was possible. . . "

It is no longer enough to plan for the predictable. We must also prepare for the unpredictable and anticipate the utterly un-imaginable. A side effect of globalism is a much higher degree of complexity and uncertainty, in addition to an already greater pace of change, impacting our lives and work. With billions of people working in an inter-connected and inter-dependent world, global innovation becomes inherently disruptive to the status quo. Case in point, Tata Motors has introduced a small car that sells for the equivalent of $2,500 (U.S.) to the Indian market.[1] Plans are underway to bring the vehicle to the U.S. for a selling price of about $8,000, after outfitting the car to meet American auto standards. Imagine the impact on compact car

A Corker of a Problem

For around 400 years, the wine cork business hadn't changed much. For centuries, cork was peeled from trees in Mediterranean countries, primarily Portugal, and then cut into cork stoppers for wine bottles. One small problem did crop up occasionally: A cork contaminated by a chemical called TCA would spoil the taste of the wine in the bottle. Enter Normacorc, LLC, with a new technology producing a plastic stopper that prevents such contamination and costs less than the traditional cork stopper. Production of the new stopper by Normacorc and other alternative cork producers has taken over 20 percent of the wine cork business. Traditional cork growers, who thought they had a lock on the market and didn't need to innovate or prepare a contingency plan, have been hit hard.—*Wall Street Journal* [2]

sales in the North American market when the Tata goes on sale in the U.S.

Worldwide systems and networks must operate seamlessly 24/7 across a myriad of environments. In many cases, "tortured compatibility" takes place as the result of a patchwork of coding and independent solutions created to make entirely different systems communicate with each other. Problems, unintentional or intentional, are inevitable. For instance, cyber saboteurs have not only stolen sensitive information that was digitally stored, but they also encrypted those files so the rightful owners couldn't even access them to assess the damage.

The sources of this global complexity, plus uncertainty and constant change are many (and the list of sources keeps growing), increasing the potential magnitude and frequency of disruptions. In a world where the improbable becomes plausible, contingency planning becomes essential. Sorry, folks, but the phrase "Nobody saw this coming" is no longer an excuse for failure!

The lesson is this: Plan to succeed (We'll call it "Plan A"), but also have an alternative plan for when Plan A goes awry ("Plan B"). *The Harvard Business Review* describes how important this is in an unpredictable world, where even the unimaginable becomes a possibility. "The contingency measures that World Trade Center tenants adopted after the landmark

Accelerators of Economic Upheaval

The following is a partial list of sources leading to more complexity, uncertainty, and change:

➢ **Data overload.** A longtime issue of complexity now compounded exponentially by Facebook and other networking tools and new sources of information, and novel digital applications.

➢ **Accelerated industry transformation.** Entire industries reinventing themselves as old business models become obsolete (examples: autos, steel, publishing).

➢ **Trade protectionism.** Trade obstructions cause dysfunction in global markets. Potential for retaliation and trade wars must be considered, especially where domestic consumer markets become less a factor in U.S. economy compared to exporting and international business.

➢ **Credit constraints.** To what extent will bank lending and other credit markets open up or be scaled back?

➢ **Debt overload and defaults.** The concern is not limited to individuals and businesses; it includes government bodies as well.

➢ **Currency stability.** The world economy is based on fiat currencies (whereby money is controlled by government) rather than on precious metals and other hard assets. As one nation after another experiences financial chaos, the value of such fiat currency becomes suspect.

➢ **Government intrusion into business and markets.** State capitalism is not the same as a free market, and creates uncertainty based on arbitrary political policies.

➢ **Disasters and accidents affecting markets.** From volcanoes, earthquakes, and hurricanes to the Gulf oil spill, markets are affected.

➢ **Wars.** The potential for disruption of markets and economies cannot be underestimated.

➢ **Demographic shifts.** Not only will the Baby Boomer bulge affect the U.S. economy for decades to come, but demographic shifts are also occurring the world over, impacting regional economies as well as global markets.

➢ **The status of the U.S. Constitution in the United States.** America redefined governance over 200 years ago. Will the Constitutional covenant with its people remain intact?[3]

1993 bombing are widely credited with saving lives and businesses in the wake of the most recent [9/11/2001] disaster."[4] The Global Innovation Age calls for entire strategies crafted to address your own worst-case scenarios.

Contingency Planning for Growth, Not Just Survival

Sometimes, it's hard to hear your cash cow *moo*-ing. Companies have one; individuals have one; nonprofits have one; and even nations have one. Whether it's a job, product, service, business unit, funding source, trade, or talent, your cash cow is what has allowed you to become successful. It's your meal ticket, the income generator that has given you the confidence to dream big, explore new interests, and expand your horizons.

Suddenly, the bottom falls out. Assumptions that were once perceived by everyone to be forever true simply evaporate. Growth and expansion are placed on the back burner. Panicky leaders, CEOs, and business owners rip their hair out, desperately searching for something that will help pull them out of the quagmire. The mantra switches from growth to survival, and everyone hopes recovery is just around the corner.

The trap too many organizations, executives, professionals, and owners fall into is forgetting about their cash cows. Once they've achieved success, they start thinking they can do anything, anywhere—or worse, they become consumed with perks, privileges, and turf wars of self-aggrandizement. They take their eyes off the cash cow in the barn and venture out in search of greener pastures.

> In the new economy of the Global Innovation Age, not only do you need to carefully tend your cash cow and the field where it grazes, but you must also constantly be on the look out for a new, aggressive breed of cows heading your way, intent on seizing part or all of your pasture and starving your cow.

Too often, what appears to be a greener pasture turns out to be a swamp. When this happens, it's time to go back to basics and focus on core products and services. Then, the prescription is to add value to those core products and services by providing extra features and services that help customers make more money, save time, and reduce their headaches.

Now, fast forward to the Global Innovation Age. Innovators from around the world (e.g., Tata Motors, in the case of autos, and Nomacorc, with wine corks) can suddenly show up with a cow that not only out-produces yours, but also delivers chocolate milk and strawberry milk shakes as well. Suddenly, their cows are taking over your pasture and starving your cash cow.

The essential lesson for survival and success in the new economy is: Waiting for events to unfold to force activation of your contingency plan is <u>not</u> enough. That's playing defense. Rather, you must go on the offense with aggressive innovation.

The above statement could justifiably be considered trite without addressing the difficulty in pursuing an "innovation offensive." The catch is how to successfully implement such an approach. Consequently, an example of organizational modeling to support such innovation is presented on the next page.

Overcoming a Certain Four-Letter Word: R-I-S-K

Contingency plans may seem like they're only for survival scenarios, but contingency planning is vitally important to support growth initiatives as well. The reason, as stated earlier, is that growth in the Global Innovation Age will require substantial amounts of innovation, and innovation involves risk. In other words, more growth entails more innovation, resulting in more risk. More risk requires a higher degree of risk management. Contingency plan-

> **More Milk from Your Cash Cow**
> Cutting costs or boosting efficiency is not enough. Every capital expenditure should also result in a customer benefit; in doing so, you leverage capital investments to produce added value.

Winning the Turf Wars

The challenge of implementing an aggressive strategy of innovation within an existing organization is illustrated by the following circles. The first circle represents the current organization. Whatever lies within the borders of the original circle (pasture) belongs to the status quo. New business development is viewed favorably as long as it takes place outside of the current organization's boundaries (in new pastures). In short, the view is "Go ahead and innovate. Just don't step on my turf."

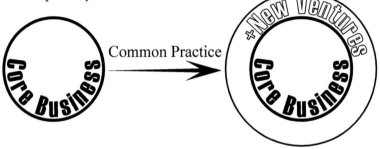

The reality is that significant innovation will intrude on the status quo's turf. The following illustration shows the reality of multiple innovations within an existing organization. Growth is not all derived from new business; some of it comes at the expense of existing business as well.

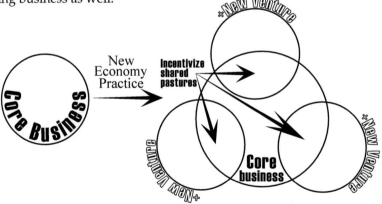

In order for such disruptive innovation to come from within an organization, the status quo must have an interest in the success of

(Continued)

> the new ventures. Often, you must create this interest, perhaps by boosting incentives for innovation and reducing the incentives for increasing existing business in current markets. Such an approach may seem counter intuitive, as it would seem to encourage taking the focus off the cash cow, but defensive actions to protect the current cash cow only buys more time in the Global Innovation Age, regardless of the quality of the fences built around your pasture.

ning is the insurance policy we issue to ourselves to mitigate the risks of innovation.

Static strategic plans that state objectives, strategies, and action plans based on a set of long-term assumptions are not sufficiently flexible given the intense rate of innovation taking place. The pace of change obsoletes many of these plans before they can be completed, or in some cases, even before they are distributed for approval or implementation.

Business plans invariably include budget estimates and the projected return on the investment based on various scenarios used to calculate the potential risk/reward ratio. Monitoring actual progress against projections and benchmarks is standard practice in large organizations. Unfortunately, in the Global Innovation Age, where entrepreneurial creativity and risk-taking is necessary, such carefully drawn budget planning may not be the best way to go about making a go/no-go decision on a new initiative.

So, how do we build contingency planning into "The Plan" so that it allows us to justify innovation when we don't know what the ultimate outcome might be? One example is an entrepreneurial technique that can be used in assessing investment in new initiatives. The focus isn't on projecting specific long-term future results, but rather on controlling downside risk while leaving profit potential open-ended.

This entrepreneurial assessment technique measures the upfront risk of rolling out a new product, service, or project.

Risk is aggressively mitigated. For example, the development and launch can be structured to minimize initial costs, such as through the use of outsourcing. Another approach would be to structure the initiative to leverage the resources of others (such as strategic alliances with critical suppliers or distributors). The contingency plan addresses what happens if the initiative doesn't prove to have sufficient potential to warrant continued support by the innovator.

The initiatives can then be rolled out quickly for market response or progress toward short-term benchmarks. Those initiatives that prove to have potential would then be acted upon, and those that don't would be quickly written off. Contingency plans to address growth when an initiative proves to have potential must also be prepared in advance and modified along the way as new information becomes available. Course changes should be expected and new initiatives may be re-invented over time. Successful contingency plans will include processes to accommodate such course changes and re-invention.

Of course, many innovations don't allow for a modest loss, but the loss is relative in that larger organizations (or those with deep pockets) can afford to take larger risks in absolute dollars. The key is to keep the investment from being too large so that losses are limited, ensuring future investment in something else. A startup company may be an all-or-nothing proposition in itself, but the investors in the enterprise should be expected to attempt to limit their losses so as to avoid losing everything they own. (And by the way, this statement is not intended in any way to disparage the untold thousands of entrepreneurs who bet everything—including their lives, at times—on making a new product, service, or real estate development a reality).

Contingency planning isn't just for survival; it's a means of supporting the innovation required to grow an enterprise in today's world. The Global Innovation Age doesn't allow for the luxury of reacting to trends *after* they are established. You must proactively move on trends *before* they are proven. Consequently, the need is great to have contingency planning systems in place as part of a strategic plan to deal with uncertainty and the unknown or unproven potential of new markets.

Is Your Business Model Obsolete?

Several definitions exist to describe a "business model," and there are countless variations. However, a simple, straightforward definition, posed as a question to describe your business model can be expressed as: How does your organization operate to deliver value to your customers and generate the revenue needed to survive and succeed? The answer to that question is your business model.

Because organizations are structured around a business model, they are slow to change, and an organization with a successful business model tends to be extremely resistant to change. After all, why fix something that's not broken?

The lifespan of successful business models is becoming shorter. A model that once operated well for decades may now be rendered ineffective in only a few years. The irony is that those organizations that have moved to a new business model based on digital capabilities may experience even shorter lifecycles of their model, as digital business models are an area of focused innovation. Think about it. We're not talking about just a few million entrepreneurs and visionaries in the U.S. inventing new business and operating methods, but rather hundreds of millions of innovators around the world with vastly different perspectives and ideas being applied to their tasks. And it's also important to remember that as the Global Innovation Age progresses, the intense pace of innovation will apply not only to products and services, but also to how organizations operate and handle money. The digital revolution is far from over.

In order to maintain a competitive edge (even in the case of nonprofits like schools, trade unions, and government agencies), you may need to make obsolete your own business model. In this regard, the contingency plan becomes "The Plan." Of course, this is the essence of the battle between the status quo of the Industrial Age trying to turn back or control the forces of the Global Innovation Age. To survive, businesses and nonprofits that don't pursue government subsidies or other preferential treatment are forced to change their business models. Other organizations that can use the power of government to pass laws and exact tax dollars from the citizenry to exercise that power and to maintain their own status quo (or minimize change for themselves) can be expected to do so.

Government will need to downsize and change its current business model, as well as its current operations in the global economy. The emerging market nations, without the established infrastructure and well-entrenched status quo and business models of the U.S., will be able to utilize the new digital technologies to leap ahead of North America in terms of how they deliver services and products.

Real-Life Example:
Old Infrastructure that Works Well
May Slow Innovation

During a trip to London in 1998, I noticed that cell phone use seemed more widespread there than in the U.S. at the time. In the UK, wait times for a landline phone to be installed could take months and phone usage costs were relatively high. North America's telephone service, on the other hand, was arguably the best in the world. The result was faster acceptance of cell phones in the UK than the U.S. because even the early cell systems represented a greater advance in customer benefit for British phone users than for North Americans.

The North American telephone industry went through years of painful adjustments before transforming itself into a digital telecom powerhouse. However, as mentioned earlier, "going digital" doesn't mean you have a business model with a nice long lifespan. For example, the established leaders of cellular phone service (AT&T and Verizon) may be facing a new threat to their business model. That threat is a consortium of thirty-four companies, stitched together by Google, seeking to turn the mobile phone into a freely open computing driver.[5] This is not a hypothetical threat; it's actually happening. Can you hear me now?

Creative destruction applies to business models as well, and the contingency plan *is* the plan in the Global Innovation Age.

PREDICTIONS	
Event	*Probability*
An outbreak of war, or acts of war, beyond the current conflicts in Iraq and Afghanistan, will rock the U.S. economy in the next ten years.	80%
Sporadic shortages of various services, natural resources and essential commodities, along with bottlenecks in supply chains—including water and electric power—will appear, disrupting lives and businesses.	80%

The Contingency Plan *IS* the Plan:
Winning Strategies for Us, as a Nation

"Business as usual" isn't going to save America in the Global Innovation Age. We are going to have to become an "innovation society" if we are going to maintain our standard of living and provide the promise of opportunity and personal fulfillment for all the nation's citizens. Toward the goal of achieving an "innovation society," certain measures must be taken:

> Create and enforce regulation in the sense of "making regular" commerce (e.g., The Uniform Commercial Code) to provide certainty in terms of contracts, property rights, and legal due process. It is essential to update laws and regulations to reflect advances in technology, processes, and the global economy.

> On the other hand, excessive, frequently changing, and arbitrary regulation and laws suffocate innovation and need to be limited.

> Reward risk-taking. Lower the capital gains rate, especially in a slow economy, to encourage taking on new risks.

The Contingency Plan *IS* the Plan: Winning Strategies for You, as a Leader

In leading your team, institute policies and programs that:

> Employ innovation as a measure of employee performance, with commensurate rewards in recognition and compensation.

> Train employees in managing project risk; particularly, define options for projects that don't develop as projected.

> Reward success but accept failure where the project was well executed with appropriate risk management steps taken.

> Ensure that contingency planning is part of your overall strategic planning.

A Contingency Plan Primer

Cash is No Longer Trash

Ah, the good ole days of easy credit! Remember when virtually anyone and their brother (or sister) would extend a line of credit to you? Those days are long gone. There will be growth opportunities—there always are—but these will be financed by more cash and less credit. Understand that your future will be dependent on your cash flow and adjust your thinking accordingly.

Prune

If cash is king, then the next logical conclusion is that all non-cash-producing products and services need to be shown the door. This is not a time for trying to squeeze water from a stone. However, there may also be some potential in retooling your product lines for customers who want more value.

"If you have the capacity in a downturn, develop a lower-value service or product that can be used to meet the needs of lower-value customers," note Reed Burton and Mark Holden, business-to-business pricing authorities. "Be very careful not to drop prices of your high-value offering, and make sure that the customers who pay the lower prices don't get access to the fast delivery or higher-quality products, even if they complain."[6]

Find the Best Customers

You have to accurately define your target market. Key to this process is identifying your best customers. These are the people who will sufficiently value what your products and services do for them and consequently be willing to pay the designated price, on time, and adhere to the terms and conditions you need.

"Remember the Preto principle," writes Hendry Lee in *Five Recession Proof Strategies*, "20 percent of your customers bring in 80 percent of your revenue. . . In a downturn, customers are more likely to go with a trusted source."[7]

While focusing on your core products and services, don't overlook your core customers while pursuing new ones. Those who have already been doing business with you are more likely to appreciate and pay a premium for what you have to offer. Of course, you have to differentiate your lines via added value features that deliver clearly discernible benefits to the customer.

The Contingency Plan *IS* the Plan:
Winning Strategies for You, Personally

Discontinuity, disruption, and creative destruction are hallmarks of the Global Innovation Age, but so are new wealth, new ideas, and better living standards for those creating and implementing innovations around the globe. You must make the extra effort to:

➢ Anticipate possible outcomes of trends and potential events.

➢ Enhance and optimize your networks, education, and finances to allow you the necessary resources to survive setbacks and implement your contingency plan.

➢ Cultivate the creativity to solve problems and work around obstacles.

➢ Develop contingency plans for yourself.

For example, anticipate foreseeable issues by reading *The Economist* and other publications that provide objective analyses of trends, and relate those trends to your personal situation. Expand your resources by networking with people who have skills that complement or enhance your own. Search in advance for specialists you may need. Develop a contingency plan for yourself that will allow you to survive if you lose your current primary source of income or if the retirement income plan you were counting on suffers major setbacks. Most importantly, you need to move quickly. Time is of the essence.

> Contingency planning is the key to avoid becoming collateral damage in the escalating disruption of the status quo by the Global Innovation Age.

Trend 2

"Brother, Can You Spare a Trillion Dollars?"

Foreign Money Will Talk ... With a Very Loud Voice

A popular song during the 1930s, "Brother, Can You Spare a Dime?" could be making the rounds once again. Songwriter Yip Harburg's lyrics, expressing pride and despair, resonate just as profoundly today as they did back then, though this time with a slight revision. Instead of unemployed and desperate men begging for dimes to support their families (believe it or not, in the 1930s, one dime could buy a Sunday paper or a loaf of bread), this time, it is Uncle Sam desperately who is seeking trillions of dollars to prop up an overextended superpower.

What began as a few subprime foreclosures and a decline in home values snowballed into an epic tale of ill-conceived financial products, bad judgment, greed, foolish political policies, and an intertwined global economy that came crashing to its knees. After plunging into a deep financial crisis, it appears the only option is to turn to foreign countries and ask them to bail us out. Uncle Sam, starred and striped hat in his humbled hand,

> **A Song for the Times**
> "Once I built a tower, up to the sun. Brick, and rivet, and lime. . . Once I built a tower, now it's done. Brother, can you spare a dime?"—Yip Harburg (lyrics), Jay Gorney (music)

has been making the rounds to foreign capitals to ask, "Brother, can you spare a trillion dollars?"

That money has, and continues to come, from the foreign nations in the form of buying U.S. bonds. Selling the bonds to finance America's spending pumped billions of dollars into our economy leading up to the crisis and allowed the U.S. to maintain the appearance of an economic superpower. We accepted the cash infusion from these countries, even though many Americans grumbled about how we were selling our future to China, Saudi Arabia, and others.

Like an overextended homeowner holding a subprime mortgage on the house with maxed-out credit cards, the U.S. government has spent too much, borrowed too much, and failed to adequately invest in the future. How did we reach this sad state of affairs? How did the United States of America—the most powerful nation in the world—turn into a subprime economy? And how did we mortgage our future to foreign countries, whose currency reserves have turned into our country's line of credit?

> **Quid Pro Quo**
> "The financial markets are going to slowly realize that the only reason foreign central banks bought treasuries is because the U.S. bought their goods first!. . . Foreign countries have no reason to buy massive amounts of treasury debt unless we buy something from them first."—*MoneyWeek*[1]

Foreign governments have been the willing enablers of this behavior. For years, America, as a debtor nation, has been borrowing money from China and other countries to finance federal spending. These creditor nations did so because it was in their best national interest. Essentially, these countries were selling to America their services and goods on credit and using their trade surplus money to buy U.S. Treasury bonds. Think of the deal this way: "You buy our goods, and we'll loan you money to keep up the spending."

Now, the foreign governments are reconsidering their investments. The world is faced with a global liquidation of debt as cash-strapped creditor nations threaten to stop accepting IOUs from Uncle Sam (or anyone else), among other measures, in an effort to protect and stabilize their own finances. If the value of U.S. Treasury bonds should plummet or the risk of such an event increases, China and other large holders of those bonds may refuse to buy more of them. This would force the U.S. to resort to printing money (leading to inflation), raising taxes (lowering Americans' take-home pay), and even more Draconian measures caused by poor planning and lapses in judgment on the part of America.

An unintended consequence of being so deeply in debt may actually buy the U.S. some time, at least in the short run. Foreign countries may feel compelled to buy our debt and eat the loss on U.S. bonds in order to protect their own economies by maintaining their exports to America. In short, this reflects a codependency whereby foreign governments buy U.S. debt and Americans buy their exports.

If Congress fails to control spending, it may be China that finally forces the U.S. government to exercise a measure of fiscal sanity in its spending spree by threatening not to buy any more U.S. debt. China is the largest foreign holder of U.S. government debt, amounting to about a trillion dollars in 2009.

Unhappy with the prospect of losses in value on that debt, the Premier of China, Wen Jiabao, has called on the U.S. to ". . . maintain its good credit, to honor its promises, and to guarantee the safety of China's assets."[2] The U.S. Secretary of the Treasury, Timothy Geithner, made a trip to China in June of 2009 to reassure the nation that the purchase of U.S. Treasury

> Final approval of the federal budget may rest in Beijing (and other foreign capitals worldwide)—not in Washington, D.C.

bonds was a sound investment. The Chinese view was essentially summed up by Yu Yongding, an influential former central bank advisor, when he said, "It will be helpful if Geithner can show us some arithmetic."[3] Mr. Geithner was cooperative and respectful toward his Chinese hosts and avoided confrontation with them on the issues. After all, America cannot afford to have China refusing to buy its bonds.

America for Sale—Rock-Bottom Prices!

With good reason, American companies, real estate, and other assets were attractive investments to foreign investors during the period between 2001 and 2008. As the U.S. dollar depreciated in value against the currencies of other nations, assets in the U.S. looked like bargains in other countries. Up until 2008, foreign investors had used their stronger currency to pay as little as sixty cents on the dollar for our assets.

American assets continue to be attractive to foreign money managers, not only because of a relatively weak U.S. currency, but also because American investment is viewed as a "safe haven." The U.S. is considered a stable, democratic country that respects property rights and the rule of law (some may argue these attributes may be compromised at this time, but compared to other countries, America is still considered the most solid on these points). In addition, the importance of the U.S. market from a global perspective drives foreign multi-national companies to invest on our shores.

> **Who Owns America?** Foreign investment amounts to one-seventh of U.S. corporate assets, based on the most recent IRS data available.—Grant Thornton International Ltd., as reported by Reuters[4]

How large has the presence of foreign investments grown? Foreign-owned companies have assets amounting to 13.9 percent of the total assets of U.S. corporations, adding up to over $9 trillion in value in 2005 (the latest year for which

IRS data is available).[5] That is a three-fold increase over the previous decade. And foreign investment is not limited to corporations. Real estate professionals report foreign investors buying Iowa farmland.[6] The People's Republic of China has relaxed visa requirements to encourage formation of Chinese tourist groups that visit America for the purpose of buying foreclosed homes.[7]

Paying Up, One Toll at a Time

To raise money, toll roads and bridges are increasingly being sold to foreign investors by government authorities. Some examples:

- ➤ Indiana Toll Road: Australian–Spanish consortium paid $3.8 billion for long-term lease.
- ➤ Virginia's Pocahontas Parkway: An Australian company bought a ninety-nine-year lease.
- ➤ Chicago Skyway: The same Australian–Spanish group as noted above purchased a lease on this tollway for $1.83 billion.
- ➤ Austin to Sequin, Texas Toll Road: A Spanish–American partnership, paid $1.3 billion for a fifty-year lease to build and operate the road.

Sovereign Wealth Funds

Besides foreign companies and private investors, most of America's major creditor nations have their own government-controlled "Sovereign Wealth Fund" (known simply as an SWF) through which they invest in the United States and around the world. What, exactly, is a Sovereign Wealth Fund? SWFs have been defined as "pools of assets owned and managed directly or indirectly by governments to achieve national objectives." The purpose of an SWF is to ". . . diversify and improve the return on foreign exchange reserves or commodity [typically oil] revenue, and sometimes to shield the domestic economy from [cycle-inducing] fluctuations in commodity prices. As such, most invest in foreign assets."[9] It is expected that such funds be invested in stocks, bonds, real estate, private equity groups, operating companies, precious metals, or other assets. In other words, it's a country's equivalent to your personal investment portfolio.

The amount of money invested in the SWFs is staggering. The Sovereign Wealth Fund Institute calculates the worldwide assets of SWFs to be in the range of $4 trillion.[10] Some analysts believe the assets could reach as much as $15 trillion by 2015.[11]

Benefits of Sovereign Wealth Funds

There are definitely benefits to foreign investment. Here is a snapshot of a few of the pros to receiving capital from a Sovereign Wealth Fund:

> **Cash in a flash:** For a growing company, capital is a precious commodity. With foreign capital, a company can initiate growth, especially when other major financing sources may be encumbered by regulations or other issues that delay funding.

> **Stakeholders, not saber rattlers**: Thomas Friedman, in his book *The World is Flat*, posited his "Golden Arches Theory of Conflict Prevention." His premise is that whenever two countries have developed a globally connected economy and a rising standard of living, as evidenced by a network of McDonald's restaurants in that country, there is simply too much to lose by going to war with each other. Further, countries that rely on trade to keep their economies flourishing will resist going to war with their paying customers and destroying their global supply chain.[12]

> **Bring on the bailout:** As was the case with the subprime lending crisis, foreign investors stepped in and provided many of our banks with a much-needed influx of cash.

Another boost to foreign investment in the U.S. has come from the concerns other governments have regarding the value of America's bonds as U.S. government spending spirals skyward. Given the choice of buying more IOUs or hard

> Foreign money in our companies is okay. Foreign money in the pockets of our politicians is not.

assets, foreign interests are opting for real estate, banks, and shares of operating companies.

You might be wondering how SWFs acquire their money. "Most of this growth stemmed from an increase in SWFs comes from an increase in official foreign exchange reserves in some Asian countries and rising revenue from oil exports."[13] As a debtor nation with a negative balance of trade, whereby the value of imports exceed exports, the U.S. has shipped exorbitant amounts of money overseas, puffing up the foreign exchange reserves of our trading partners. Now, our trading partners are

Money Can't Buy You Love, but It Can Buy You Influence

Money can't buy you love, but it can bend the ear of a government official. Consider some of the numbers:

➤ During a recent six-year period, foreign companies spent $620 million on lobbying elected officials.

➤ In recent years, there have been approximately 1,700 lobbyists (over three lobbyists per member of Congress) representing more than 100 countries before Congress, the White House, and the federal government.

➤ Lobbyists can earn seven-figure salaries, and there are almost 250 former Congressmen and senior government officials who are now active lobbyists.

—*The Independent* (UK)[14]

using those funds to buy U.S. assets at bargain prices. The profits from SWFs are generally intended to help fund their own nations' retirement and healthcare systems. Consider the irony, as our government continues policies that will compromise the retirement and healthcare of American seniors.

With this tremendous amount of wealth comes a lot of influence, especially on Capitol Hill. For many public officials, working for foreign governments in a lobbyist role has become the equivalent of a retirement income. After years of public service, you could call this "the Beltway Pension Fund."

At first glance, it may seem un-American to allow or condone substantial foreign ownership of U.S. assets. However, generally speaking, SWFs and other foreign owners have been responsible long-term investors, providing the capital our country needs. Foreign investment actually helped build our country. In the 1800s, the British and French invested heavily in the United States, providing us with much-needed capital to fuel growth. Today, foreign investment provides vital capital for U.S. financial markets.

What needs to be considered is transparency, whereby foreign investors disclose holdings, strategies, management, and ownership, especially SWFs. Some SWFs, like Norway, Singapore, Ireland, and Chile, already meet high standards of transparency, while others provide little information. More transparency should help alleviate suspicion on the part of the American public regarding SWFs and mitigate demands for protectionist policies.

Gushing Cash

On the next page is a list of major SWFs, listing the associated country and assets of each. Take a close look at the Source column to see the primary origin of their investment capital.

Major Sovereign Wealth Funds		
Country	**Assets $ Billion**	**Source**
United Arab Emirates	738.9+	Oil
China	732.5	Non-commodity
Saudi Arabia	436.3	Oil
Norway	395	Oil
Singapore	332.5	Non-commodity
Russia	219.9	Oil
Kuwait	202.8	Oil
Hong Kong	193.4	Non-commodity
Libya	65	Oil
Qatar	62	Oil
Algeria	47	Oil
Australia	42.2	Non-commodity
Kazakhstan	38	Oil
Brunei	30	Oil
France	28	Non-commodity

— Data from Sovereign Wealth Fund Institute (Accessed June, 2010); table by author

The Threat of Global Debt Defaults

The financial struggles of Greece, Italy, Ireland, Portugal, Spain, and other countries related to managing their national debt (known as "sovereign debt") is more than a matter of curiosity to Americans. After decades of spending freely, the sour global economy is bringing the ability of countries to service their debt into question. Default on sovereign debt isn't anything new and can be clustered regionally around the globe. The world is globally intertwined financially. Just as the collapse of Lehman Brothers reverberated around the world, so would the default of a major country or a series of defaults by smaller nations disrupt economies around the globe.

Is major sovereign default a realistic concern? According to Kenneth S. Rogoff, PhD and co-author of *This Time Is Different: Eight Centuries of Financial Folly,* financial crises make sovereign debt default likely.[15] The United States, Germany, and Japan, the richest nations in the world, may not be able to fund substantial sovereign bailouts to minimize economic damage due to their own financial troubles.

PREDICTION	
Event	*Probability*
Foreign ownership of U.S. companies and assets will grow as other countries prefer to buy hard assets rather than U.S. bonds. Government bodies will sell toll roads and other assets to raise cash.	90%

Japan, the world's second largest economy, may be close to default itself. After trying to spend itself into growth for two decades through massive public spending, the country has a plunging savings rate, aging (and declining) population, and a current trade account balance in an extended downturn. Yet, the nation's political leaders are seemingly unable to wean themselves from an addiction to spending and borrowing. If major sovereign debt defaults spiral out of control, the impact in the U.S. could include:

➤ Currency devaluations against the dollar, making U.S. exports more expensive in foreign markets. Successive rounds of currency devaluations could occur as troubled countries try to gain advantage with their trading partners.

➤ Taxes likely to go up, up, up, as the U.S. would have to raise the money from its citizens rather than borrow from other nations who are tapped out financially or hoarding cash.

➤ Inflation is also likely to result as countries crank up their printing presses and try to inflate away the value of their debt.

> ➤ Global economic depression.
> ➤ Austerity programs, resulting in massive cutbacks in government services to the public.
> ➤ Higher borrowing costs.
> ➤ Volatile stock and bond markets.[16]

"Brother, Can You Spare a Trillion Dollars?": Winning Strategies for Us, as a Nation

Foreign governments have poured countless dollars into the U.S. but only because they've enjoyed profitable returns. Anxious about the value of the U.S. currency falling due to inflation and other economic policy failures, foreign governments are using the U.S. dollars they receive from exporting to America to buy assets and resources in the U.S. America's public officials need to put the country's financial house in order and initiate pro-growth economic policies NOW, before potential sovereign debt issues force extraordinary austerity measures and/or inflation takes over.

America needs foreign money, and engaging in protectionist policies is self-defeating. Requiring a greater degree of transparency from SWFs is in everyone's best interest. The issue of sovereign debt is not much different than for individuals and families. The nations with cash reserves and solid finances will enable their companies and investors to turn any foreign sovereign debt crisis into opportunity.

> **Bucks, Not Bombs**
> A powerful argument in favor of Sovereign Wealth Funds (and foreign investment in general) is that nations that engage in substantial cross-investment with one another generally avoid going to war with each other. After all, bombing your own factories, shopping malls, and office buildings is a lose/lose proposition. Moreover, nations that invest heavily in each other are more likely to partner in defending and protecting those assets.

"Brother, Can You Spare a Trillion Dollars?":
Winning Strategies for You, as a Leader

For a leader, especially in a business, SWFs and other foreign investors can offer a world of opportunity. Every organization needs capital to grow, and foreign countries are a source of potential funding. If you're going to look overseas for your capital, you must understand the basics of international banking and economics.

Foreign investors could become one of your best sources of capital. They're looking for growth, and because of their enormous reserves, they may be more patient with long-term prospects. With the increased political outcry for transparency, they may also be more passive investors, giving you the control you need to run your organization effectively.

"Brother, Can You Spare a Trillion Dollars?":
Winning Strategies for You, Personally

Learn a foreign language—or two or three! Learning two foreign languages will differentiate you from others and open up more opportunities. You don't have to be thoroughly fluent as long as you know enough to be polite, order a meal, and travel without an interpreter.

Take a class on international finance and learn the basics of currency conversion. Even better, attend a workshop or seminar at a foreign school with English language classes. The London School of Economics, for instance, offers a range of programs for extended off-campus learning, short-term studies, and executive education.

Your understanding of Sovereign Wealth Funds and foreign investment in the U.S. should also help you find the best potential employers. If you're in the job market, don't overlook companies with solid foreign ownership. You may well find the work environment to your liking.

Trend 3

Healthcare on Life Support

Will You Recover?

In 1979, the topic of my master's paper was the healthcare cost crisis. I focused on the rising costs of medical care. My research pointed to dysfunctional government healthcare policies complicated by contradictory demands of health insurers, medical providers, and many patients themselves. Three decades later, I'm disappointed to report that essentially nothing has changed in this regard—with one notable exception.

That exception is the extent to which the debate on healthcare policy has become ideologically driven. Facts are twisted, ignored, or denied. The propaganda machines are turned up to high speed to rationalize and promote each special interest's viewpoint.

In the meantime, the proverbial 800-pound gorilla stands just outside the door, ready to move in and crush the squabbling inhabitants living within the U.S. healthcare system. Namely, the Medicare hospital trust fund is projected by the U.S. Trustees

The combination of reduced Medicare payroll taxes due to recessionary times and the arrival of the Baby Boomer generation into the ranks of those covered by Medicare (beginning in 2011) has pushed the projected insolvency of Medicare to 2017.—Social Security and Medicare Boards of Trustees, 2009 Annual Reports[2]

for Social Security and Medicare to be insolvent by 2017.[1]

The Patient Protection and Affordable Care Act of 2010 (also known as "PPACA" or "Obamacare") will likely aggravate rather than alleviate the precarious financial condition of Medicare. For example, this law reduces the Medicare budget by nearly half a trillion dollars, despite the financial stress Medicare is already struggling under. Medicare participants have been assured that the difference will be made up by rooting out fraud and waste in the system. Somehow, this claim would be much more credible if the budget cuts were on a dollar-for-dollar basis after the unspecified cases of fraud and waste were identified and eliminated.

The Big Picture

The U.S. medical system has available some of the most advanced technologies, treatments, and therapies in the world. From biotech to medical devices, America remains the global innovation leader in healthcare.

Yet, according to a 2007 report by the Commonwealth Fund, "Despite having the most costly health system in the world, the United States consistently underperforms on most dimensions of performance, relative to other countries."[3] Further, thousands of people file for bankruptcy each week because they are unable to pay their medical bills.[4] Millions of Americans can't obtain the insurance coverage they need because of pre-existing conditions or because they cannot afford to pay the premiums.

It's not that the two main participants running the show— the government and the private sector—haven't been trying to figure out ways to improve the system. Rather, it's that they've too often neglected the most important part of the equation: YOU, the patient. Ultimately, *you're* the one—along with your doctor—with the most power to help the system work wisely and keep costs under control. After all the years of failed political promises, skyrocketing costs, and gaps in healthcare coverage, you must take a shot at becoming part of the picture. How? By stepping outside the realm of traditional health insurance practices.

A Short History Lesson

Won't the latest round of healthcare coverage reforms fix the problems people have in terms of affordability, insurance coverage, and timely, high-quality care? Political fixes based on "top down" controls and mandates rather than "bottom up" patient-doctor choice invariably involve political expediency, resulting in unintended consequences that usually wind up undermining the very intent of proposed reforms. This shouldn't be too surprising. No two human beings are exactly alike, especially when it comes to health and medical care. Mammoth one-size-fits-all solutions have a difficult time achieving timely, cost-effective, high-quality care tailored to individual needs.

Consider the federal government's landmark effort at expanding healthcare coverage: the introduction of Medicare in 1964. At that time, *Time* magazine reported that Medicare advocates believed the "measures would bring enormous health benefits to millions over sixty-five, covered by Medicare, and to more millions in low-income brackets who would be covered (states permitting) by Medicaid."[5]

They were right. More people were covered than ever before, but the program upset the economic laws of supply and demand (substantially increasing demand for medical services without a commensurate boost in supply of medical providers) and other market mechanisms (patients were largely insensitive to costs, as they were paid by third parties). *Time* magazine also noted: "Partly—although not entirely—because of the plans, hospital costs are soaring at the rate of 15 percent a year, double the previous rate. Doctors' fees are edging up, a dollar here and a couple of dollars there. Many physicians are doubling their incomes while staying within the law. The overall costs of both Medicaid and Medicare are running astronomically higher than pre-enactment forecasts."[6]

Attempts by the government to cap Medicare reimbursements (and by health insurers to control costs) resulted in cost shifting, such as doctors seeing more patients to make up for lower reimbursement rates or increasing charges to private payers to offset lower Medicare fees.[7] The additional regulations and requirements for authorizing expenditures and obtaining reimbursement added to the administrative cost burden for medical providers.

The escalating costs caused health insurance to grow increasingly expensive—and therefore less affordable—to average Americans and their employers. Medicare also crowded out the private health insurance market for seniors that existed before passage of the new entitlement. The private sector could not compete with the taxpayer-subsidized government healthcare program. Today, the Medicare program is more expensive than ever. "Total Medicare spending exceeded half a trillion dollars in 2009."[8] The only larger categories of federal spending are Social Security and defense.

Medicaid, the joint federal-state program designed to help low-income people with their healthcare needs, is also a budgetary behemoth. Even though federal dollars fund the lion's share of Medicaid, the program still typically takes up an estimated 16.8 percent of a

> A side effect of cost controls by third-party payers has been for some medical providers to engage in cost shifting, whereby unreimbursed patient costs are passed on to other payers.—Rutland Regional Medical Center (which provided an online example of cost shifting)[9]

state's general fund budget, on average. Under PPACA, this percentage will grow even higher. According to the Georgetown University Health Policy Institute Center for Children and Families, "Medicaid is the largest single source of healthcare coverage in the nation."[10]

Let's look at the private sector's involvement, which picked up speed during World War II. At that time, wage and price controls were in effect due to the war effort. Employers were able to offer expanded tax-deductible employee benefits to attract and retain the workers they needed. However, the tax deductibility of health benefits was not extended to individuals, and employer-sponsored health insurance became the politically favored option for healthcare coverage in the U.S.

After the war, America was in the prime of the Industrial Age. Upwards of one-third of all employees were in unions, working for big industrial companies that paid the cost for generous health insurance coverage. Insurance coverage costs were generally acceptable for group plans. However, in the sunset of the Industrial Age, as the population aged, the range of covered health services expanded, more expensive medical technological advances became available, and costly government regulations grew. Not surprisingly, so did health insurance costs.

Increasingly, employers reported difficulty keeping up with rising employee health coverage costs. According to a PricewaterhouseCoopers survey of 291 CEOs, "Most fast-growth private businesses claim to have suffered an impact from higher health costs over the past twelve months."[11]

In 2009, President Obama declared healthcare to be the number one issue to be dealt with by the country. As part of the extensive political process leading toward legislation, three basic approaches, with a virtually infinite number of variations within each, were proposed and debated: a market-based system relying on private insurers for catastrophic events, with greater emphasis on the insured paying more of their own medical costs through higher deductibles (generally known as "direct pay"); a national or government-run healthcare system ("single payer"); and a status-quo modification system amounting to maintaining the prevailing third-party reimbursement of healthcare costs.

A market-based, or direct pay, approach focuses on the objective to provide the insured with more choices at lower costs by increasing competition and patient cost sensitivity. Common characteristics of this approach include:

> Permit individuals and employers to purchase health insurance across state lines. This would allow interstate commerce for customers looking for health insurance policies and dramatically increase competition. Also, it would allow for larger pools of people with pre-existing conditions to be covered.

> Encourage formation of Health Savings Accounts, which would allow individuals to save for medical costs over time, just as an IRA does for retirement costs.

> Enact tax credits to cover the cost of insurance premiums and/or deductibles for individuals and families to purchase their own insurance policies.

> Rein in malpractice litigation to reduce the cost of "defensive medicine" practiced by medical providers to mitigate malpractice lawsuits.

> Provide vouchers for those with incomes below a certain threshold to pay for out-of-pocket medical expenses.

A market-based direct pay approach has downsides: This approach assumes the insured population has the requisite education and resources to make appropriate choices (a problematic issue for many who are sick, disabled, elderly, and others with limited education or language skills). The cost and availability of insurance coverage for pre-existing conditions and catastrophic illness for the elderly, the unemployed, the independently employed, and those moving to another job or state remain subjects of debate. Finally, the temptation of politicians to continually increase voucher amounts and mandate benefits for the poor will be no less than the government-mandated increases in benefits and coverage experienced in the Medicare program.

A national healthcare, or single payer, system is another approach, whereby the government would act as the insurer, pay all the costs, and cover everyone. Advocates of national healthcare plans, with few exceptions, ask: If other countries like Great Britain and Canada provide universal healthcare, why can't the U.S. do the same? However, seldom have the national healthcare advocates acknowledged the enormous trade-offs with such a system.

In both countries, Canada and Great Britain, we're seeing byproducts of national healthcare that none of its proponents want to talk about: limited access and lack of availability of convenient, state-of-the-art medical equipment and devices. Let's start with Great Britain. They recently passed a law in which emergency room (ER) patients must be seen within four hours—yes, FOUR hours. To relieve potential overcrowding from this new, "tight" restriction, ambulances have been allowed to sit outside the ER for up to five hours with a patient BEFORE admission to ER, where the patient could sit and wait for up to another four hours.[12]

Access to healthcare is a problem in Canada, according to Canadian author and doctor David Gratzer. In a scathing indictment of the Canadian system, he wrote, "I soon discovered that the problems went well beyond overcrowded ERs... Patients had to wait for practically any diagnostic test or procedure, such as the man with persistent pain from a

Woe Canada
A group of Canadian doctors opened up their own private clinics to provide timely access to care and services not provided by government facilities. The clinics were closed by the government, which led to a legal challenge. The verdict by the Canadian Supreme Court? "Access to a wait list is not access to care." The doctors won.

hernia operation whom we referred to a pain clinic—with a three-year wait list; or the woman needing a sleep study to diagnose what seemed like sleep apnea, who faced a two-year delay; or the woman with breast cancer, who needed to wait four months for radiation therapy, when the standard of care was four weeks." [13]

Any version of mandated universal care that adds tens of millions of people to the healthcare insurance rolls will aggravate a system already struggling with severe shortages of doctors and nurses.[14] Government regulation and direction of the care delivery system would inevitably lead to government control of the education, training, and income of doctors and other medical professionals. A national healthcare system that provides all medical services in a high-quality manner in a timely fashion to everyone at no charge will resort to some sort of rationing of benefits, usually in the form of long delays, in order to serve the demand and control costs.

Do we want a system in which the government ultimately decides who is qualified to receive care, what type of care, and how much care? Are we ready to have a committee decide based on a cost-control standard that a twenty-six-year-old man should receive cardiac surgery but not a seventy-year-old woman, without regard for the individual circumstances and with little recourse by the patient?

Two valid counterarguments to the preceding paragraph are:

> Ability to pay or qualify for insurance coverage should not determine whether a patient receives necessary medical care or prescription drugs.

> Healthcare is already rationed or dispensed to a certain extent based on cost/benefit assessments by many insurance companies and medical providers.

Both of the above counter-arguments are sound reasons for reforming America's current system for covering healthcare costs, but they are not reasons to replace the current system with one that may be worse in many ways.

In the end, America wound up remaining with a government-influenced, third-party reimbursement system when PPACA was passed during March 2010. Politically divisive with onerous regulations and taxes, the public, both the political right and left, have expressed their distaste for the legislation, even though for different reasons (the left wanted a single-payer public option, and the right objected to the government intrusiveness). The new law injects substantial complexity, uncertainty and change into an already troubled economy and constitutes a case study on Industrial Age thinking in the Global Innovation Age.

The claims that the new law will allow people to keep their present health plans and reduce overall healthcare spending are open to question. The "grandfathering" of present employer-sponsored healthcare plans has already been compromised by government direction after passage of PPACA. Henceforth, the grandfathering clause will only apply to those plans where the employer sponsor does not switch to another health insurer or substantially change the terms or cost of the plan. The budget projections for PPACA are premised on critical assumptions, including the following:

> ➤ Health insurers are able to absorb the cost of providing greater benefits while having insurance

Losing a Few People for the Greater Good
A federal advisory board recommended in 2009 that women under the age of fifty forego routine mammograms. This recommendation was based on the fact that relatively few women develop breast cancer before that age, so the cost/benefit wasn't deemed justified—unless, of course, you happened to be among the thousands of women with the misfortune to develop breast cancer at a younger age. In response to public outcry, the U.S. Health Chief stated the mammogram recommendations would not be implemented. However, public concern that such advisory boards would inevitably wind up having the power to set such guidelines under the PPACA has not been dispelled.—U.S. Preventive Services Task Force via Agency for Healthcare Research and Quality and CNN.com[15]

premiums limited by the government and will not exit the business.

➢ Increased taxes on "the rich" and businesses will not impact economic activity negatively and tax revenue to support the new programs will climb as projected.

➢ The government will manage healthcare programs better than the private sector.

Whether the PPACA will work as promised comes down to the validity of the above assumptions. What is your opinion on these assumptions?

Regardless of whether you believe the PPACA is a step in the right direction or not, you need to start or step up your participation in a powerful trend to work around the shortcomings of the healthcare system. Read on to find out how.

The direction is for individuals to be more aware and responsible for the costs of their own healthcare. With information sources and new services rapidly developing to meet individual needs, we're on the brink of seeing healthcare redefined whether or not the PPACA of 2010 winds up intact or modified or repealed. Proactive and educated individuals will increasingly direct their own healthcare and circumvent the faults of the American healthcare system.

The Patient Must Become Part of the Equation

A major trend emerging in the healthcare world involves the rise of the individual. It's you, the patient. Rather than relying on a third party to see to your health needs, you're going to have to become more involved in your own health and the health of your family. As you'll see with many of the new programs, the choice is a rather narrow one: Either you decide to get healthy, or you'll start paying more for your healthcare and/or settle for what someone else feels your life warrants. Here are some examples of how this is already happening:

(Continued)

Incentive-based Plans

A healthy lifestyle has become an important element in employee benefits. More employers are offering wellness programs, encouraging employees to stop smoking and lose weight, such as:

- ➢ Adopting no-tobacco policies on and off the job.
- ➢ Offering cash-incentive payments and gift cards.
- ➢ Reimbursing workers for gym memberships.
- ➢ Providing free health coaching.
- ➢ Offering insurance premium discounts to those who meet health standards, and surcharges to those who don't.[16]

Why are employers doing this? Because it works. When employers become involved, costs decrease, and healthy employees stay on the job.[17] Some examples of wellness initiatives being implemented by companies follow:

- ➢ Safeway reduces healthcare rates for employees who don't smoke or undergo a heath risk assessment.
- ➢ IBM pays employees $150 to $300 to exercise or quit smoking.
- ➢ Northeastern Log Homes lowers health insurance premiums for employees who meet with a health coach and participate in exercise programs.[18]

Digital Answers

Besides involving you with cost-savings measures, you're now in a position to address many of your own medical questions. People are now frequently turning to the Internet for their information to assist them in making their own healthcare choices. "Eight of ten Internet users have looked for health information online, with increased searches in: diet, fitness, drugs, health insurance, experimental treatments, and particular doctors and hospitals," according to the Pew Internet & American Life Project.[19]

A Booz Allen Hamilton study of nearly 3,000 adults and 600 physicians revealed that health consumers:

- ➢ Who have greater cost responsibility are more aware of cost and quality differences, but are only beginning to act upon this information and "shop" for value.
- ➢ Who have plans with health savings options (such as health savings accounts) appear more willing to spend now to avoid potential health complications later.
- ➢ In general, expect medical providers to compete primarily on quality; health plans to compete on price; and drug companies to compete primarily on price, but to a slightly lesser degree on quality.

(Continued)

(Continued)

In the same study, physicians had a different perspective:

➤ Less than 20 percent believed consumerism would produce better health outcomes or better patient-physician relationships.

➤ Many feel consumer-directed healthcare will have a negative impact on patients.

➤ Fifty-eight percent believe patients will limit their use of necessary healthcare services and procedures.[20]

The increase in health-related searches on the Internet indicates that more people are looking for digital information to make better health decisions. "Eighty percent of Internet users, about 113 million adults, have researched a health topic online."[21]

Healthcare Coaches/Advocates

As individuals become expected to handle their own costs, they'll need help. We turn to accountants for our taxes, financial planners for our investments, and now we'll be turning to healthcare coaches, or advocates, for our medical care. The coaches help employees compare and contrast plans, access benefits, and troubleshoot claims. They'll also help select doctors and hospitals, address provider network issues, and tackle doctor/patient communications issues.

A firm offering healthcare coaching, Health Advocate, Inc., saw its client list double from 800 to 1,900 within a two year period. CareCounsel in California is banking on continued future growth as well. "I think it really will become a mainstream benefit because so much is driving it," said CareCounsel CEO Larry Gelb.[22]

Rating Hospitals and Doctors

If you're going to be expected to manage your own costs, you'll need to become a better healthcare consumer. Just as *Consumer Reports* gives you the lowdown on the best autos, appliances, and electronics, evaluations are also being conducted on our healthcare system. A service named Angie's List (www.angieslist.com) has started consumer ratings of "A" to "F" for doctors.[23]

This new trend is in its infancy, but its growth is inevitable. Many new databases are being created that grade physicians and their hospitals (including one managed by Medicare). In the past, such access has generally been restricted to healthcare providers, but that practice is changing

(Continued)

Medical Tourism

For the wealthy, curbing healthcare costs isn't even an issue. They can simply choose to bypass the system entirely. One such example is medical tourism. Why pay an exorbitant amount of money for a surgical procedure when you can travel abroad and receive exceptional care at a fraction of the cost?

"Medical tourism is growing and diversifying. Estimates vary, but McKinsey & Company and the Confederation of Indian Industry put gross medical tourism revenues at more than $40 billion worldwide in 2004. McKinsey & Company projects the total will rise to $100 billion by 2012," reports the National Center for Policy Analysis.[24]

Alternative Medicine

Expect growth in treatments outside traditional medical care. These include chiropractic care, acupuncture, Chakra healing, neuro-massage, homeopathic and herbal remedies, and others. Such treatments may be in conjunction with—or in lieu of—traditional Western medicine. Alternative medicine will provide a ready source of relief for those who are unable to obtain the care they need or when they need it from traditional sources.

Pay-as-you-go Medical Care

Instead of allowing insurance companies or the government—via Medicare and Medicaid—to direct costs and procedures, medical practices have sprung up that refuse to take such reimbursement and are paid directly by the patient. In these cases, the patient and the doctor make the medical decisions. The primary market is affluent families who can afford the out-of-pocket costs of routine care while protecting themselves from huge medical costs with high-deductible catastrophic insurance policies.

Self-directed Healthcare

Just as retirement plans have moved in the direction of defined contribution and employee-directed 401(k) plans and away from defined pensions directed by third parties, the same is happening in healthcare. In short, people are managing more of their own healthcare rather than relying on their employers' plans to cover costs. Expect to shoulder a larger share of the cost. Higher deductibles, higher premiums, larger co-pays, and more restrictions on allowable coverage, amounting to thousands of dollars a year for participants, are fueling the move to patients exercising discretion on their lifestyle, preventive care measures, and the type of medical care they need.

PREDICTIONS	
Event	*Probability*
Americans will increasingly seek medical treatment outside the U.S. Medical tourism will become a global growth industry.	90%
The Patient Protection and Affordable Care Act will not make it to 2018 as it is currently written. The law will be amended in substantial ways or even repealed and replaced.	95%
The Patient Protection and Affordable Care Act will not brake rising healthcare costs. Expect total healthcare expenses for insured individuals and families, on average, to rise after factoring in premiums, deductibles, co-pays, and out-of-pocket expenses for services not covered by insurance plans.	85%
Alternative medical treatment will grow in popularity as conventional medical care becomes more expensive, less accessible, and more impersonal.	80%

Healthcare on Life Support:
Winning Strategies for Us, as a Nation

The Industrial Age template of Big Business, Big Government, and Big Labor with paternalistic policies providing generous lifelong healthcare benefits has given way to a new reality. The Global Innovation Age has forced employers to dismantle their costly infrastructure in order to keep expenses in line with uncertain revenue streams. Public officials, armed with the power to tax, have generally considered the government exempt from the economic realties faced by the private sector. However, state and local governments are now feeling the same brutal economic realities that the private sector faces. In time, the federal government will follow suit.

The issue in the U.S. is affordability of high-quality healthcare services. Practical solutions from the political arena continue to elude us. Why shouldn't we be able to purchase health insurance across state lines? Why shouldn't the Federal Employee Health Benefit Program (FEHBP) that members of Congress enjoy be expanded to all Americans? How will we provide health coverage for all the Baby Boomers that qualify for Medicare without bankrupting the country?

Waiting for someone, somewhere, to do something that resolves America's healthcare coverage issues is not a promising Plan A. The Plan B is personal empowerment for people to control their own healthcare future.

The FEHBP is not experiencing the severe financial crunch faced by Medicare. The bureaucracy running it is limited and, unlike Medicare, does not try to set prices for doctors and hospitals. As a form of "managed competition," it offers choices of modern benefits and private plans to federal retirees (and active workers) that are unavailable in Medicare. In fact, the program offers the widest selection of health plans in the country. Comprehensive information is provided to enrollees. A completely different payment system is used, blending a formula with negotiations to achieve a remarkable level of cost control while constantly improving benefits and enjoying wide popularity among participants.

> **Benefits for the Beltway**
> Congressional leaders are enrolled in the Federal Employees Health Benefits Program (FEHBP). "It (FEHBP) outperforms Medicare in service, benefit generosity, fraud prevention, and protection from catastrophically high healthcare expenses."
> —Walton Francis[25]

Healthcare on Life Support:
Winning Strategies for You, as a Leader

Healthcare benefits, from insurance to gym usage, are valuable tools for attracting and retaining the talent you need for your organization. In fact, for many employees health benefits may be a greater factor than pay, especially semi-retired Baby Boomers. Companies that embrace this shift will be big winners.

Employers are in a unique position in that they can demonstrate the effectiveness of allowing workers to influence healthcare costs. As employers use more and more incentive-based programs (such as exercise, weight loss, and smoking cessation) and witness the health of their employees improve as a result, further systemic changes can be implemented that will further empower individuals. If you can find a way to offer greater healthcare options for employees—particularly in regards to their choice of coverage—you will create a significant recruiting and retention carrot.

Healthcare on Life Support:
Winning Strategies for You, Personally

Get ready, because change IS coming. If you've gotten this far in this book, you know that already. You're about to become more involved in your health choices than ever before. It's time to develop an understanding of what it takes to become healthy and commit to that lifestyle. If you abdicate all responsibility and turn to the government or your employer to take care of your medical needs, prepare to sacrifice access and/or quality of care.

Regardless of what Congress does on any healthcare legislation, you will still be directing your own healthcare. In a sense, you will be self-insured up to a certain limit, as out-of pocket expenses climb due to higher deductibles, co-pays, and restrictions on coverage for the specific kind of care you prefer or may require. You will need to work around the system by engaging in medical tourism, using alternative medicine, and incorporating personally directed programs into your health planning.

Trend 4

China Stands Up

Will We Live in the Shadow of the Red Giant?

In a previous business, I imported Christmas tree ornaments. As you might guess, this was a seasonal business. The merchandise was designed in the U.S., and production was labor intensive, as each ornament had to be handmade. The only way we could create viable profit margins was to outsource production with specialty manufacturers in China.* Essentially, this allowed us to utilize the low-cost labor force in that country.

This type of managerial maneuver was supposed to be a nobrainer for the bottom line. Cheap labor equals increased profits, right? For the most part, that arrangement proved true. We did make money off the inexpensive imports, and the model proved effective, but there were also plenty of headaches.

Our biggest problem with Chinese imports was the inconsistent quality. Whenever we accepted a container shipment of merchandise, we never quite knew what would be awaiting us

---

* Whenever "China" is mentioned in this book, the reference is to mainland China, also known as The People's Republic of China, and not The Republic of China, commonly known as Taiwan.

inside the box. Would there be a number of crushed and broken ornaments? Would we find a series of mismatched colors and poor paint jobs that would make the items difficult to sell? Our answer wouldn't come until the crowbars hit the crates, and on numerous occasions, we ran into problems.

When we did find some problems, we were stuck. Because we accepted shipment of the merchandise in September with the holiday just around the corner, we really had no choice but to accept the merchandise as-is. In America, a flawed order of Christmas ornaments might be replaced and reshipped before you could sing "Oh, Tannenbaum," but with our overseas friends that possibility simply didn't exist. We had to take our flawed delivery and write it off as a cost of doing business with a low-cost labor market. You get what you pay for, especially when dealing abroad. That's the way the jingle bell crumbles.

In truth, the Chinese did not set out to ruin my Christmas. They actually performed relatively well once the smoke cleared and the broken ornaments were swept away. The point of my Christmas story is that despite conventional wisdom that proclaims China will rule the world, this colossus is not invincible. America is not necessarily destined to live in the shadow of the Red Giant.

In many ways, the fear factor regarding the arrival of China on the global market is remarkably similar to the rise of Japan in the 1980s. "Japan, Inc." was feared because the country was united in its desire to become the world's reigning economic superpower, but Japan never materialized into the overpowering force it was purported to be. There's no denying Japan is still a major player in the global market, but it is not the "king of the mountain."

Comparing Today's China to Yesterday's Japan

History doesn't repeat exactly, but it does carry some striking similarities. Today's China has some similarities—and striking differences—with the Japan of the 1980s:

Differences:

> **High-tech, excellent management:** China today is not as advanced in terms of its high-tech prowess and management expertise as was Japan of the 1980s.

> **Foreign investment:** China welcomes foreign investment. In 2004, direct foreign investments in industries like auto reached nearly $55 billion, while Japan's was only $8 billion.

> **Backed by the USA:** The U.S. economy is heavily intertwined with China, and China encourages foreign investment. Japan was more restrictive in terms of foreign investment.

> **Opposed by the USA:** While we were at odds with Japan economically, we never opposed their political structure. China's Communist regime and relations with countries like Iraq and the Sudan have created tension.

Similarities:

> **Similar ascents:** Like Japan, China's rise was based on exports, focusing on strategic industries like auto and electronics. A recession in the USA could severely hurt China, as it did Japan in the '80s.

> **Currency quandary:** Both countries have faced pressure to strengthen their currency to help reduce a huge trade deficit with the U.S.

> **Bubble in property values:** At its peak, Japan had a real estate bubble with its coastal cities. After the bubble burst, the country felt the pain. We're already seeing a similar pattern developing in China.[2]

The China of today is an even more intimidating force than Japan was in the 1970s and '80s, primarily because of its imposing size. In terms of the world population, one out of every five people lives in China. The country has an enormous

China's Free Trade Agreement with Southeast Asia
After a six-fold increase in economic activity over the previous decade with the countries who belong to the Association of Southeast Asian Nations (ASEAN), China announced a free trade agreement with this group, scrapping tariffs on about 90 percent of goods. The U.S. was not included. The ten-member nations of ASEAN are Indonesia, Thailand, Malaysia, Singapore, Brunei, the Philippines, Cambodia, Laos, Myanmar, and Vietnam. China and ASEAN nations represent a quarter of the world's population.
—*The China Post*[3]

labor pool—skilled and unskilled—willing to work for lower wages and fewer benefits than workers in the Western world. They have also exhibited a desire to engage in the world marketplace, reaping the rewards of their competitive advantages and slowly becoming more conciliatory in their political dealings, except when it serves their interests to take a strong position.

China's leadership doesn't have to think in terms of election cycles. The focus is long-term, looking out twenty years, even fifty years. Their goals are rarely stated explicitly, but their actions certainly imply that. China intends on taking a leadership position in the world.

Consider the following:

> China is forming its own trade alliances with countries, without U.S. involvement.

> The U.S. dollar, currently the world's reserve currency, is gradually being reduced as a holding in China's currency reserves. Instead, China has introduced a basket of currencies and gold to back up its own currency which could eventually be independent of the U.S. dollar.

> China's military is growing mightily. The objective appears to have a military commensurate with the country's economic and political clout.

While there is no denying China's competitive advantage in the present, there are plenty of signs of potential weakness in the future. Several underlying elements jeopardize China's rapid growth and objectives (see the next page).

China's Vulnerabilities

Marginal Margins
China has insisted on valuing its currency at a rate lower than the prevailing market rate of the U.S. dollar, resulting in lower-priced Chinese exports in the U.S. While this approach has helped sell more commodity products, the downside has been that Chinese exporters have typically received lower prices for their goods. As China has grown and experienced greater demand for natural resources and basic materials, those costs have risen, along with labor costs, as the economy has expanded. Consequently, commodity manufacturers tend to have thin margins and weak balance sheets. If an uptick in costs occurs, perhaps as a result of rising labor costs, higher electric power charges, stricter environmental standards, or new safety measures, millions of jobs will be lost as businesses cut back.

China's manufacturing base has been upgrading to more added-value production. An example is the Chinese battery maker, BYD, which has been moving beyond its roots as a low-cost producer of batteries to a world-class innovator. In addition, China has significantly strengthened its banking system. What is anyone's guess is whether China will win this race against time to build a financially stronger private sector that can withstand economic storms before an economic downturn deflates asset values there.

It's in the Air
Environmental conditions are a serious problem for China. Air pollution is a serious concern in several regions to the point that citizens don surgical masks as part of their daily routines. According to the Council on Foreign Relations, "sixteen of the world's twenty most polluted cities are in China" and "one-third of the nation's population lacks access to clean drinking water."[4]

The environmental problems have not gone unnoticed by the world community. "The [Chinese] government received 600,000 environment-related complaints in 2006," the Council on Foreign relations reported, ". . . a figure that has risen roughly 30 percent each year since 2002."[5] This kind of uproar will eventually spur action on the part of the Chinese.

China Has a Skills Shortage
A real challenge for China to grow in the global economy has to do with its university education system that produces too few

(Continued)

(Continued)
graduates with the skills necessary to work for foreign companies in the country, specifically the many Chinese companies seeking to become global enterprises. According to a McKinsey & Company report, fewer than 10 percent of the nation's university graduates have the practical training and language skills suitable for employment at companies with world-class standards.[6]

China's Speculative Bubble May Burst
China's fast-growing economy has sparked speculation in land and other assets. Total outstanding debt, including off-balance-sheet liabilities, is approaching 70 percent of Gross Domestic Product (GDP). For the sake of comparison, debt and obligations are approaching 50 percent of U.S. GDP. Big developers are highly leveraged and dependent on low interest rates and rising prices to support their projected payoffs.[7] *Forbes* magazine described the situation with these examples:

> ". . . government bureaucrats funding themselves by foisting debt on state-owned enterprises; local governments raising capital by selling land to corporations they own; and a People's Bank of China lavishing liquidity on the entire system in a way that makes Federal Reserve Chairman Ben Bernanke look downright stingy."[8]

Other issues will need to be resolved, and some of these are just as daunting as the ones detailed here: China's insatiable energy and power needs and the abuse of copyright laws and patents. China's stand on human rights and the repression of a society, especially in an era when information is ubiquitous and gobbled up by a curious population, just won't stand after a strong middle class emerges.

China has some powerful forces on its side, like its annual current account surplus of over $2 trillion. If everything goes as planned, the country could grow out of its problems. If not, well. . .

Finding Work in a Chinese Factory

In cities and towns around the U.S., thousands of American

workers are aleready employed at Chinese-owned factories. The gap between manufacturing costs in China and the U.S. is narrowing in an array of industries. Faced with higher wages, material costs, land prices, and electric power charges in their homeland, Chinese manufacturers are increasingly eyeing opportunities to set up shop in the U.S.

Other factors are also encouraging such moves. American states, ports, and municipalities have sent representatives to China offering tax credits, cheap land, and abundant, reliable, low cost electric power to entice Chinese companies to locate operations in America.[9]

Meanwhile, the Chinese government is offering an investment tax credit for companies to place factories in key overseas markets. Government support like this makes sense on the premise that the Chinese currency is likely to rise in value over time as compared to its Western customers, making Chinese exports more expensive.

Even so, won't the cost to manufacture low-tech, commodity-type products remain lower in China than in the U.S.? Probably, especially where the manufacturing process is labor intensive. However, when indirect costs are considered, the picture changes. By strategically locating factories in the U.S., Chinese manufacturers can provide their customers more reliable delivery, lower inventories, better quality control, better communication, and enhanced access to parts and service. Finally, the "Made in America" label helps sales, especially when American-made products are required for government contracts.

Moving to America	
Chinese manufacturers with operations in the U.S. include:	
Company	**Products**
Tianjin Pipe Group	Oil drilling pipes
Top-Eastern Group	Tools/drill bits
Haier	Appliances
Yuncheng Plate Making	Printing label cylinders[10]

PREDICTIONS	
Event	*Probability*
General Motors will make more money, or claim it could make more money, from Chinese-made automobiles than from U.S.-made automobiles.	80%
China will influence American policies with its power to impact commodity markets, financing of U.S. debt, and the U.S. dollar's status as the world's reserve currency.	90%
Low-priced automobiles manufactured in China will threaten U.S.-based auto manufacturers.	65%
China may experience an economic crisis—or at least a recession. The global ramifications would dwarf the U.S. economic problems of 2008–2009.	65%

Besides complexity, uncertainty, and constant change, the new economy, reflecting the Global Innovation Age, has its share of irony as well. These are the seeds of the Age of Global Convergence yet to come. Those with a negative perspective will claim that China's entrance into the global market will put extra strain on America's ability to compete globally. Critics will also point out that trading with a country known for its civil rights abuses is a contradiction for the United States, considering its emphasis on individual freedom. As China continues to connect and become even more intertwined with the global economy, it will feel the pressure to loosen the reins on its own people. China is, indeed, an increasingly powerful colossus, but one far from perfect.

China Stands Up: Winning Strategies for Us, as a Nation

Tactically, James A. Dorn, China specialist and co-editor of *China's Future: Constructive Partner or Emerging Threat?* recommended the U.S. government engage the Red Giant in the following ways:

> ➤ **Continue the strategic economic dialogue** initiated by Presidents Bush and Hu Jintao.
>
> ➤ **End the discrimination against China** in anti-dumping cases by recognizing China as a market economy and admit the country to the G-8 (a group of the eight most highly industrialized nations that meet annually to address global issues) as a normal rising power. These two acts of friendship would reassure Beijing that the United States welcomes China's rise and does not view the Red Giant as an inevitable enemy.
>
> ➤ **Don't ignore the human rights violations that occur.** Use diplomatic pressure to help move China toward a legitimate rule of law.
>
> ➤ **Uphold the same market-liberal principles** it wants China to adopt. By adhering to a free-trade agenda, the U.S. government can show the Chinese people that Americans practice what they preach.[11]

In a larger sense, America must define itself differently if it's to avoid living in the shadow of the Red Giant. Zachary Karabell, author of *Superfusion: How China and America Became One Economy and Why the World's Prosperity Depends On It*, explains that reinvigorating America's economic life is the key: ". . . America needs to re-tool its domestic economy to build on the global success of many U.S. companies. It must focus on inventing new products and generating new ideas rather than defending the rusty industries of yesterday."[12]

China Stands Up: Winning Strategies for You, as a Leader

The reality is that China is not an omnipotent force. It has been a player in the global marketplace for years, and we've already seen American businesses adapt in many ways. The key is to focus on your strengths—such as exceptional supply-chain management, intellectual capital, customer focus, and sales savvy—and use them to penetrate the pots of gold around the world.

China houses one-fifth of the world's population, and it is proving to have an insatiable appetite for American brands and celebrities. During the 2008 Beijing Olympics, basketball star Kobe Bryant created a sensation that rivaled the 1964 arrival of The Beatles in the U.S. Young Chinese are increasingly on-line, hot for the latest in electronics and media. You may have noticed by now that the rules of the Global Innovation Age are different from that which you are accustomed. Address China's potential but have your Plan B ready.

China Stands Up: Winning Strategies for You, Personally

So, what can the average American do? First, continue your ef-forts to professionally keep ahead of the "Joneses" of China, India, and other countries. Don't measure your job skills by do-mestic standards; think about how you stack up *globally*. You can and should set the bar at a professional skill level far be-yond what's available in China. Understand where America will have a competitive advantage, and train yourself to be suc-cessful in those industries.

Second, keep close tabs on how China is approached by your bankers, consultants, and other professionals. Are they aware of the potential growth for companies who can figure out how to tap the Chinese marketplace? Are they taking the necessary steps to ensure you can survive in the event China enters a period of turmoil?

Third, plan a business or personal trip to visit China and as much of Asia as you can. See firsthand China's place in the world, with your very own eyes.

Fourth, consider sponsoring a foreign exchange student or intern from one of the BRIC countries (Brazil, Russia, India, China) as a positive step toward cultural outreach and understanding. Also, enroll in an adult education class or attend a seminar on the subject of Chinese culture, language, current events and/or business development.

Fifth, you can easily invest in China without leaving home. Numerous exchange traded funds (ETFs) and mutual funds are available that provide a basket of shares in Chinese companies as part, or all, of their holdings. However, investing in Chinese securities carries significant risk and you should seek competent professional advice before doing so.

Finally, Chinese companies and investors have been buying into U.S. companies and real estate markets. The larger of these transactions can usually be tracked down on the Internet. You may come across some great investment or career opportunities worth pursuing.

> **The Golden Rule**
> "Who has the gold, makes the rules. And China is on a headlong path to accumulate as much gold as it can. China is now the world's largest producer (miner) of gold, and all the gold mined in China must be sold to the government. What in the world could the Chinese be planning? Here's what I'm thinking. The yuan will become the world's most wanted currency, heavily backed by gold and a stable government, plus the planet's biggest military. In due time, China will be the new owner of the world's reserve currency."—Richard Russell, Legendary Investment Newsletter Author and Investor[13]

Trend 5

The Employed, the Under-Employed, and the Unemployable

A Split-Level Workforce: Two Floors and a Basement

The couple next door is worried. At first glance, you would think there was no cause for alarm. The couple, whom we'll call Bill and Bev, are in their early fifties, and both appear ready to enjoy life as empty-nesters. They have lived happily in their neighborhood for years, held down reliable jobs, and have basically enjoyed the American Dream.

Bev is an insurance claims specialist. She works in a large company, taking claims over the phone and processing them. Bill works for an equipment manufacturer. He performs a variety of jobs that arise in the service area, from checking in equipment for repair to coordinating work with the mechanics. They perform very well at work, meeting all the job requirements and performing their duties with diligence and a sound work ethic. Both Bill and Bev are caring, conversant people who are friendly, honest, and exceptional neighbors. They work hard, own their home with the help of a thirty-year mortgage, and enjoy the simple pleasures of life.

So, what's worrying Bill and Bev? The problem isn't with their past, but with their future.

Let's consider Bill and Bev from a career perspective. In the context of today's economy, their resumes have some issues. Neither has a college education or a specific trade skill. Both have worked for one company for the majority of their lives, and both perform relatively routine jobs that could be outsourced to lower-wage workers or eliminated by a restructuring of job duties among the workers.

Bill and Bev are part of a split-level workforce that's emerged in America, and they're mired on the level that's in deep trouble. The two of them have spent much of their lives cruising along American Dream Lane, built and maintained by the Industrial Age economy. It was an economy that allowed people with relatively few skills to enjoy good pay, good benefits, a home in the 'burbs, and two and a half kids, all with a forty-hour work week. Already, there are signs that Dream Lane is getting rougher and bumpier for Bill and Bev and others just like them.

Last year, Bill and Bev almost lost their home when Bill was laid off. His company has been bought and sold three times in the past ten years, and with every buyout his job status grows shakier. New hires are paid substantially less than the starting pay long-term workers received. For Bev, the future is equally uncertain. Consider the actions of a competitor to Bev's company: They recently moved their entire claims department to Texas, where they can hire workers at significantly lower wages to do the same work.

The handwriting is on the wall, and the split-level workforce has emerged. It will be a windfall for the highly skilled

> **Same Job, Lower Pay**
>
> In January (2010) Ford Motor Company announced that it would add 1,200 jobs at its Chicago assembly plant but didn't trumpet that the new workers would be paid half of what current workers were paid when they began. —Robert Reich[1]

professionals living on the upper floor, but for many good, hardworking people like Bill and Bev, it's a staircase down to a lower standard of living.

The Split-Level Workforce: The Trend

The effects of the split-level workforce can be distilled into a single sentence: In America, we have millions of jobs that employers are unable to fill, and we also have millions of workers who are unable to find a job.

Sounds crazy, doesn't it? But it's happening right now, and in the future it's going to happen more and more. The Industrial Age jobs are fading away while millions of American workers lack the training and flexibility to qualify for the new types of jobs being created in the post-Industrial economy.

America has become a split-level workforce with two floors of workers. The upper floor consists of the "people with skills" and the lower floor consists of "people without (or with only limited) skills." For the people with skills, the globalization of commerce, advancements in technology, and need for a highly skilled workforce pose a world of opportunity. For the people without skills, the technology-driven globalized economy amounts to the iceberg waiting to sink their ship.

The resulting income and employment gap is widening between the skilled and the unskilled (or limited skilled). At the end of 2009, a university study found that the "Great Recession" of 2008–09 affected those at the bottom 10 percent of the income scale far more than those in the top 10 percent. The study stated that "the relative size of the gap in unemployment rates between workers in the bottom and the top income deciles was close to ten to one."[2]

> "Too many job seekers lack the necessary higher skills of literacy, experience, education, and specialized career training needed for an increasingly sophisticated world of work."— Edward Gordon[3]

Education and Unemployment

Unemployment rate in 2009

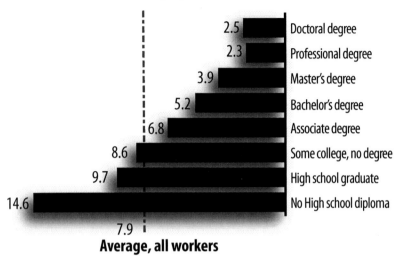

2.5	Doctoral degree
2.3	Professional degree
3.9	Master's degree
5.2	Bachelor's degree
6.8	Associate degree
8.6	Some college, no degree
9.7	High school graduate
14.6	No High school diploma

7.9
Average, all workers

–Bureau of Labor Statistics Current Population Survey

Now, you may be thinking, "Just a minute. The labor market is no walk in the park for people with skills right now either. There are unemployed IT professionals and folks with doctoral degrees driving cabs, among other skilled people unable to find the kind of jobs they have trained for." In an intensely competitive and uncertain economy, technical skills have developed a shortened life cycle. In addition, they may need to be enhanced or coupled with other skills (such as interpersonal skills, for example) to meet changes in the business and work environment. Simply attaining "geek" status is no longer an assurance of a good job. Becoming a "super-geek" or developing the people and communication skills to become a technical consigliore is required.

Possessing the right combination of skills and expertise matters more than ever, and employers are seeking out the people with skills. Manpower, Inc., issued a list of the hardest-to-fill jobs based on a lack of job candidates with the necessary skills:

Real-Life Example:
Cruise Control Is Great for a Car, Not a Career

My father was a sales engineer who designed and sold automation systems. For years he enjoyed a prosperous life, complete with flexible hours and a comfortable lifestyle. He was cruising along just fine until the Japanese entered the market.

He saw the threat coming but figured he could maintain his status quo with a "Buy American" approach and thus avoid relocating or making a career change that would interrupt his lifestyle. In short order, the new Japanese machine tools priced him out of the market. Because he worked on straight commission, he lost two-thirds of his income within a year. Caught unprepared, he lacked the educational credentials needed for the job market at that time and was unwilling to return to school. In his early fifties, Dad felt it wasn't worth it to return to school or learn a new trade. He spent the rest of his life moving from job to job, just barely making ends meet.

It was difficult to watch, but it instilled in me a valuable lesson: What you have built or created over a lifetime can be lost very quickly. In today's globally competitive economy, you can't coast along in cruise control. You must rely on your skills instead of resting on your laurels.

Manpower, Inc.'s 2010 List of the
Five Hardest-to-Fill Job Positions in the U.S.

1. Skilled Trades
2. Sales Representatives
3. Nurses
4. Technicians (primarily production/operations or engineering
5. Drivers[4]

Note that these positions are not restricted to white-collar professions. The common ground all these positions share is that they require some sort of specialized training.

Similarly, the "gift of gab" isn't enough for a sales representative to be successful in the new economy. The ability to analyze customer needs—which may be highly technical or complex—is

**The Winning
Combination**

"Another reason employ-
ers are having a tough
time filling some jobs:
the growing need for
workers with uncommon
combinations of abilities,
such as communications
and people skills plus
technical knowledge."—
The Kiplinger Letter[5]

essential. The knowledge to understand and explain complex financial transactions and legal instruments or the intricacies of technically complicated equipment, systems, or designs in a manner to which a customer can relate requires a high degree of skill and training.

People with skills may experience nasty potholes in the labor market, but the situation will be progressively downhill for people without skills. You can see the fallout every day. Tune into your local newscast, and you'll hear a report about a paper mill or an auto manufacturer laying off thousands of people. In most cases, the displaced workers are people without a high level of skills, the ones whose repetitive job functions are either being automated or shipped out of the country so the company can ultimately save money.

And we can't blame the plant owners for the decision; the marketplace forces the decision. As much as employers might like to pay employees more and provide them with that cozy house in the suburbs with the two-and-a-half kids and swimming pool, they can't. You can't fill anyone's swimming pool if the revenue well runs dry.

The Industrial Age economy model, based on Big Industry, Big Government, and Big Labor, provided a comfortable level of compensation, structure, and stability for people without skills, but that era is now gone, and these people are being dumped on the street without an adequate safety net.

Down in the Basement: America's Unemployables

An on-going, unresolved problem is the increasing number of high school dropouts, now amounting to over 1.3 million a year, contributing to the creation of an "underclass" in America.[6] If high school graduates *with* a few valuable skills are finding it tough going, imagine the difficulties facing this rapidly expanding underclass. This part of our society is especially prone to—or a product of—the problems of crime, drug and alcohol abuse, and dysfunctional families. According to the Alliance for Excellent Education, the social programs, jails, and medical treatment programs this population requires will soon cost our economy three *trillion* dollars.[7]

> ". . . three out of every ten students failing to earn a [high school] diploma represents a legitimate reason for concern. But by the same token, the fact that barely half of students educated in America's largest cities are finishing high school should truly raise an alarm among those who care about the future of public education and the nation as a whole."[8]

By creating or allowing this huge underclass to exist outside our mainstream economy, we are rotting the very foundations of our society. This underclass may lack the skills and ability for holding down even the most elementary of jobs and not have role models to help them find a way up and out of the basement. Besides the societal cost, the immorality of allowing failed public education systems to mire millions of Americans in a life of unfulfilled potential has real (and lasting) effects on our society. Efforts at long-term reform aimed at addressing these issues are laudable, but millions of people are lost along the way.

The Pressure Will Continue to Build

For America, the development of the split-level workforce is going to force some tough decisions. As the people without skills grow frustrated watching their job prospects and standard of living decline, tremendous pressure will be placed on government agencies to provide services, but without the funding necessary to support the measures.

Real-Life Example:
The Gap without a Bridge

The gap between the workforces described in this trend is complicated by the fact that there is no easy way to bridge the divide. A
home healthcare worker who hailed from three generations of welfare recipients was the first one in her family hold a job. Even with
three daughters and no husband, she was able to make ends meet
because of her eligibility for food stamps and healthcare.

It is an inspiring story, but because of the political framework
of the social welfare program, it's one that ends there. This woman
was unable to take her career to the next level because her eligibility
for these social programs was limited and threatened by her income.
When she reached a certain income level, the benefits were phased
out, including medical and dental care coverage for her and her
children. To advance beyond making what was a meager income
to sustain four family members would have been financial suicide.

This anecdote is meant to serve as an example of a program that
fails to provide the necessary bridging mechanism for our country's
citizens. We have systems that allow people to reach plateaus when
what we truly need are social programs that facilitate a climb to daz-
zling new heights.

Contrary to what you might think, this decline is not restricted to large urban areas either. Many small rural communities are
already in a state of perpetual decline. According to a report by
the Carsey Institute covering a six-year period, " . . . 1.5 million rural workers lost their jobs due to fundamental changes in
industries that have historically been the mainstay of the rural
economy."[9] It's a sad but simple truth that low-skill jobs are leaving the small towns they have supported for years. The people
who do have skills are leaving, too, heading elsewhere for better
pay and greater opportunities.

Whose fault is it? It is unproductive to play the blame
game, and no one specific instance has caused the situation.
It's been a steady mixture of a welfare system, failing public
schools, crime, broken families, and poverty. We have no

national policy that addresses the problem effectively, and we most likely can't reverse course in time to prevent harm to the future millions of students in failing major urban school districts. Now is the time to make radical changes.

PREDICTIONS	
Event	*Probability*
Unionization will grow among the ranks of workers in low-wage service jobs with few or no benefits, but long-term union membership growth in the U.S. overall won't be significant.	70%
Large numbers of those who have had their benefits, pay, and entitlements cut—along with crowds protesting taxes and government policies—will march on state capitals and Washington, D.C.	90%
The trend toward adult children moving back home at times because they can't afford to live independently won't abate.	80%

The Employed, the Under-Employed, and the Unemployable: Winning Strategies for Us, as a Nation

Addressing the split-level workforce will involve a change in perspective, and it starts with marketable skills. There are no good alternatives. Relying on collective bargaining agreements for the unskilled/semi-skilled to achieve gains in the workplace offers limited hope. The labor movement is up against the forces of globalism for its industrial membership and the beginning of an era of government downsizing that will reduce public sector jobs. Use of the Internet by consumers to shop, source, and trade goods and services will limit the long-term gains for union members in the retail sector.

Attempts at reforming public education, from vouchers to charter schools and now the "Race to the Top" program, have experienced limited implementation due to the power of the status quo and the Industrial Age model of schools as education factories. Unfortunately, at this late date, any radical change will come at the expense of one group or another.

Simply pouring more money into the current public education system without an overhaul of strategic direction and the use of educational technologies will only perpetuate an obsolete approach that doesn't prepare students to be winners in terms of global innovation. Most public school teachers strive to provide the best possible education for their students. However, like dedicated employees in a declining business with an uncompetitive business model, they resemble the *Titanic* crew members who stayed at their posts, diligently and loyally doing their jobs until the frigid waters of the North Atlantic swept them away.

The starting point has to be with failed schools. Time has run out to allow troubled school administrations second and third chances to work out their problems. Issue vouchers to allow parents with children in failed schools to send their children to the school of their choice. Upheaval like this won't be without mistakes, but we have to go beyond the status quo and move on to solutions. Also, we need to take on students who want to drop out of high school. Fund and scale up successful programs to keep students in school (such as those sponsored by America's Promise and other organizations).

Our country faces a huge challenge in providing the training and education necessary for workers to become owners of a basket of marketable skills. Employers need to be an intrinsic part of the process, as do vocational schools and technical colleges. Subsidies for workers to acquire skills and tax credits for employers to pay for training workers are needed.

> Each year, the total number of high school dropouts represents $330 billion in lost lifetime earnings.—Alliance for Excellent Education

The Employed, the Under-Employed, and the Unemployable: Winning Strategies for You, as a Leader

Businesses today are caught between the proverbial rock and a hard place. The rock lies across the ocean, where legions of skilled professionals and low-paid frontline workers provide global competitors a substantial commercial advantage. The hard place is here in America, where there are not enough people to fill all the skilled positions and not enough positions for all the people without skills.

What's a beleaguered leader of an organization to do in an economic and social state like the one in which we find ourselves now? One option is to pack your bags and move the plant overseas. But, if you're not ready to throw in the red, white, and blue towel, then Plan B is to initiate your own training programs, either online, through outsourcing, in-house, or in conjunction with a local education institution such as a community college.

Real-Life Example: Where Did All the Supervisors Go?

Speaking from personal experience as a CEO, one of the more difficult types of positions to fill (even during a recession!) has been first-level supervisory positions. In the new economy, such positions require pre-learned management skills that many people don't possess. The structure and layers of management in large Industrial Age companies that enabled people without skills to work themselves into such positions generally don't exist anymore, as companies have streamlined their workforces to the bare minimum. Conversely, people with skills who have graduated from a university have been reluctant to take such jobs, as these jobs are viewed as a level below their education and career expectations.

You should also look at innovative ways to recruit. You'll need to reevaluate your recruitment and compensation program to find new ways to step up your approach. Benefit programs will have to change, and you'll find yourself bending over backwards to provide flex-hours and unique work arrangements. It may be necessary to develop the skill sets your organization needs in-house with the staff you have rather than recruiting additional staff. Consider tuition and seminar reimbursement programs to encourage existing employees to develop new and better skills.

The Employed, the Under-Employed, and the Unemployable: Winning Strategies for You, Personally

If you are one of the people with skills, you're in a good position—provided you are staying ahead of the competition by networking, applying your knowledge to generate productivity increases, and diversifying your skill base. Some ominous signs on the horizon should keep you from becoming complacent:

> First, make sure your skills stay sharp, because while your talents may be in high demand here, the marketplace may look overseas for solutions. Countries like India and China are making it a national priority to produce more engineers—professionals who may come at a cheaper price tag than American-grown talent.

> Keep pushing the intellectual envelope, and watch your company's performance. Only smart American companies will find a way to stay afloat in this increasingly competitive market, and you'll need to make sure you're on the right team.

> Outside the workplace, you and the rest of society will face plenty of challenges as well. The town you live in may be suffering from a lower tax base as people lose jobs. The quality of your public schools may be on the decline, and you may be forced to move your children to private schools. The social malaise creeping throughout

society will touch you—will touch all of us—in some way or another.

Don't wait to acquire new skills until you are unemployed. For anyone who is unskilled, a "temporary" break in employment may very well mean that job is permanently gone.

Developing new skills may seem an overwhelming prospect, so approach it one day at a time. Visit a local vocational school or college recruiting office and discuss career prospects. Consider your own skills: Where do your talents lie? What kind of training do you need to take yourself to the next level? Be creative and active, but most of all, be independent. You may think you can't afford to make these moves, but the straight-up truth is that you can't afford not to.

Trend 6

America's Spending Binge

We're in for a Lingering Hangover

The Law of Unintended Consequences may lead to an economic upheaval that reduces the standard of living for many, if not most, Americans. The law states that for every action taken, unintended consequences can derail the intended outcome. This is certainly the case in the United States as it faces deficits and commitments in the trillions of dollars that it can't possibly fund without damaging the economy. The problem is not limited to the federal government. State and local governments are feeling the stress as well. If a stone is thrown into a pond, it will produce ripples. A giant boulder, not a stone, has been rolled into the United States economic pool, and the impact threatens to capsize the nation.

How Could this Happen?

Didn't America win the Cold War and become the sole superpower in the world? Since World War II, the world economy has been based on credit, with the United States leading the charge (no pun intended). The credit binge extends into the halls of government, in which entitlements, wars, and bailouts have been slapped on the nation's plastic. Consumers who routinely carry a credit card balance in the pursuit of life, liberty, and a big-screen TV have duplicated this behavior. Access to cheap, easy money created by the Federal Reserve encouraged banks to lend liberally. Businesses were encouraged to leverage up based on "pro-forma" projections of future earnings, not current cash flow. After all, borrowed money was cheaper than equity funding.

Politicians became increasingly predisposed to the notion that there were few limits or negative consequences to expanding government programs or imposing controls, complexity, taxes, and liabilities on the private economy. As power shifted to the public sector, so did the flow of money. Budgets in the millions of dollars grew to billions and then ballooned to trillions. Inevitably, political influence became an ever more valuable and necessary investment. Trillions of dollars in the public pot has attracted the intense interest of lobbyists. The politically connected and political wannabes have lined up to dip their spoons for a taste of the jackpot.

As the unintended consequences pile up from excessive spending and political gamesmanship, the pressure will be on elected officials to spend still more money to paper over the mistakes and deficits. How will such spending be funded? The federal government can fund its spending five ways: tax, borrow, print money, dispose of assets, and confiscate property. State and local governments fund their spending the same way, with the exception of printing money. The possibility of seeing most, if not all, of of these ways taking place is likely. The end game has the potential to further compromise market mechanisms to operate effectively, throwing America's entire economic system into peril.

Waging wars . . . bailing out the nation's largest banks . . . taking over auto manufacturers . . . borrowing money to fund an enormous stimulus package . . . subsidizing and (possibly) nationalizing healthcare . . . expanding entitlements . . . taking on climate change . . . micro managing the economy . . . paying out the retirement benefits owed to a huge demographic group known as the Baby Boomers . . . shoring up pension funds . . . stationing military personnel in over 100 countries. No country can do all of these things at once, particularly one that's short of revenues. The spending habits of a superpower are about to crash and burn, and with that we'll see (and quite possibly feel) a very different economic paradigm.

> "Can the West, with its regulated industry, labor, and large government, afford its borrowing-funded living standards and increasingly expensive public sectors?"
> — Roland Nash, Chief Strategist at Renaissance Capital [1]

In the pursuit of short-term profits in the private sector and political expediency in the public sector, business and government leaders have focused on patching over symptoms in order to buy time. Despite Herculean efforts dwarfed by anything done previously in U.S. history and despite the reassurances of economic advisors and political leaders, the outcomes are anything but predictable. The "unintended consequences" that follow are not predictions, but possibilities that may result from excess spending and the economic and political expediency currently afflicting America. Yet, among the potential dire circumstances that seemingly await a pensive American public, there is hope. American history is an operatic story of looming disaster averted in unanticipated, improbable events orchestrated by daring leaders.

War without End

The wars in Iraq and Afghanistan have reminded the world what should have been learned in Vietnam: There is no such thing as a "small war" or a "contained conflict." Wars are incredibly costly in lives, sacrifice, and treasure. They are also incredibly dangerous and can escalate.

From the pirates of Somalia to the mullahs of Iran and the terrorists of the Taliban, there doesn't seem to be a shortage of tyrannical regimes presenting potential conflicts in the world at any given time. When war takes place, it must be treated as a nation's number one priority and not simply another government initiative. There are not sufficient trillions of dollars available to fund all of the social programs, entitlements, stimulus packages, bailouts, and other spending the politicians have promised *and* fund a winning war effort without damaging the U.S. economy.

The unintended result? A war effort that drags on, sufficiently funded to keep troops in action, but not the single-minded focus of effort and resources to finish the job successfully. Withdrawal from the war theater may remove most U.S. soldiers as an act of political expediency, but American funding of the government and surrogate military forces left behind in war-torn countries would invariably continue.

Policies that place American men and women in harm's way and do not dedicate every resource, and commit whatever funds are needed, to win the war decisively and as quickly as possible, should be viewed as immoral and unacceptable. At the time of this writing, American soldiers are sacrificing life and limb in Iraq and Afghanistan. Families of those who die will carry the weight of those losses forever. The wounded who do return will suffer silently in pain. Domestic political agendas cannot be allowed to trump or distract from the war effort from a moral as well as a practical standpoint.

> A war has to be a nation's number one priority, not just another agenda item to be juggled among other spending initiatives.

Stimulus Spending Is Just the Down Payment

Spending on unnecessary construction based on political considerations will result in carrying costs and maintenance expenses that will linger on well after the construction is completed and the immediate economic benefit has faded away. The drain on many local and state governments for the continued costs of upkeep will be significant.

In addition, stimulus funding doesn't sufficiently address the need to upgrade America's digital infrastructure to provide a competitive edge in the new global economy. As James Carlini, network infrastructure expert, stated, "Antiquated processes, network infrastructure, and information systems create just as many liabilities as old and rusting bridges and crumbling roads with deep potholes."[2] In other words, too much stimulus spending has been directed at maintaining the past rather than preparing for the post-industrial future. The resulting costs of an inadequate digital infrastructure in later decades will be profound.

Overspending for projects, waste, and outright fraud, along with political pork for favored special interest groups will only aggravate the debt that all Americans will be obligated to pay off at some point. This debt will be paid back in the form of higher inflation and/or taxes. The American public will likely be increasingly repulsed by the massive corruption and waste, resulting in an ever-growing popular movement that will demand that the government clean up its act.

Another potential—albeit unintentional—consequence to consider is that the stimulus, despite the corruption and waste, may coincide with an economic recovery or the flood of money will inflate asset values, creating the illusion of recovery. Unfortunately, the politicians would likely credit their actions with such a recovery and be unable to resist returning to their previous practices and thrust the country into another round of economic malaise.

Cash . . . with Strings Attached

The government has pumped trillions of dollars into the financial system not only to bail out specific companies and industries, but also to prop up the economy in general. But such money comes with strings attached. In this case, the financial support translates into more regulation and control of the economy on the premise of protecting the interests of the taxpayers.

From licensing tax preparers to compensation guidelines for companies that took bailout money and much more, everyday life in America is becoming more regulated. A growth industry may well be found in helping organizations and individuals fill out government forms and facilitating the process required to gain permission to do just about anything, or to obtain benefits.

Credit More Expensive, Less Available

Attempting to undo the damage from the subprime loan debacle, massive bailouts of banks and the "autonomous" federal mortgage corporations (commonly referred to as Fannie Mae and Freddie Mac) were launched by the federal government. Along the way, bankers, private lenders, bondholders, and other creditors have been vilified as greedy vultures preying on unsuspecting debtors. Chrysler and General Motors bondholders found their legal rights to be abrogated by the government's Auto Task Force, placing the interests of the unions and government ahead of long-established bankruptcy principles. Creditors of mortgages faced demands that mortgage contracts be modified in favor of those who had mortgaged their homes to the hilt and were unable to make the required payments. The bailout funding came with politically inspired conditions that punished those receiving the money, with many of the strings attached retroactively. Interest rates charged by credit card companies and other lenders drew the ire of politicians as well. The justification for such actions was that the financial crisis required extraordinary action, along with a desire by politicians to appear as though they were on the side of fairness and taking care of the "little guy."

Naturally, banks became gun-shy about the bailout money or even lending money, for that matter. Lenders and other creditors fretted about their rights and having government controls imposed on lending. The intent of the government was to re-liquefy the financial system and jumpstart lending, but why would any lender or investor part with hard-earned dollars if the government can supersede established lending laws, limiting creditor rights and financial returns?

The unintended consequence is for potential lenders—whether bankers, institutional lenders, or private investors—to lend only to the most credit-worthy people and companies. The amount of money lent will be less, as a percentage of the total value of the collateral. Lenders will also charge higher rates to offset the increased costs of greater regulatory compliance and not only market risk, but also political risks in lending money. Americans (and companies) with lower incomes and credit ratings will find the amount of money available to be borrowed from the private sector quite limited, with onerous terms and much higher interest rates. Those in the bottom quartile of income and credit scores will

> **Tracking Transactions**
> Another example of the link between higher government expenditures and increased regulation: The Patient Protection And Affordable Care Act includes a provision requiring an IRS form 1099 to be filed on virtually every business transaction over $600. The stated reason for this massive surveillance is to reduce unreported income and therefore enhance tax revenues to defray costs of the new 2010 health-care law. The result will force millions of businesses to take on the time, cost, and liability of issuing hundreds of millions, perhaps billions, of these forms. For instance, if a self-employed person buys a computer costing over $600, he/she will have to obtain the vendor's address, Social Security number, or business tax number, and issue a Form 1099 to both the vendor and the IRS.—CNNMoney.com[3]

The Wall Street Reform and Consumer Protection Act of 2010 will burden lenders with more costly regulations and further restrict flexibility of the financial system. find it extremely difficult to obtain credit on any terms as Congress imposes ever more regulations and limits on bankers. Such limits on lending will lead to more unintentional consequences by serving to slow economic recovery and consolidate economic power into the hands of larger banks and companies.

Higher Taxes for All

Where will the money come from to pay for the trillions of dollars to be spent by government bodies? State and federal politicians claim the middle class won't pay more and only the "rich" will face higher tax bills. In fact, a higher tax burden will invariably fall hard on lower- and middle-income Americans, including those whose incomes are so low they don't even have to file an income tax return. Why? Congress, state legislatures, and local governments are feverishly devising and raising new taxes, surcharges, and fees on just about every product, service, and activity imaginable.

States don't necessarily tax all services currently. Expect this to change. Utilities, from electricity to garbage collection, are big potential revenue sources. Nevada, for instance, is considering extending its 6.5 percent sales tax to natural gas. Wisconsin intends to increase its recycling tipping fee, environmental management tipping fee, and environmental repair fee on solid waste dumped into landfills. None of the Wisconsin increases will go toward environmental issues, but into the general fund. Washington (the state) wants a levy on streetlights. Maine, Illinois, and Michigan are sizing up telephone answering services, temp agencies, health clubs, and lawn mowing as potential sales tax sources.

Expect new state and local tax levies on beer, soda, cigarettes, gas, garage sales, car/boat/RV/motorcycle registration fees, sporting events, the use of parks, fishing, hunting, and just about anything else a person might touch or do. New taxes and fees on businesses amount to an indirect tax on the public, as such additional costs are, to some degree, passed along—either in higher prices and/or lower quality and less quantity in products and services.

More insidious are the duplication of taxes by multiple government bodies. The federal government taxes telephone and cell phone services, and as do states and even some local governments. The attitude seems to be, "If another government body is taxing something, why shouldn't we?"

Government Services Scaled Back

After nearly thirty years of downsizing, restructuring, and utilizing technology to become more efficient in the private sector, the public sector will begin to follow suit, albeit with a lot of kicking and screaming. As state and local governments can't print money to inflate their way out of debt like the federal government, and where their finances reach a point when no one will loan them money, raising taxes (and fees) to unprecedented levels (and/or back scaling government programs) is the next recourse.

For example, California voters during May of 2009 rejected five referendums boosting sales, use, and income taxes. The response from state government officials was to announce cutbacks in government services.[4] In many cases, such cutbacks won't be the outright elimination of programs but will instead appear as increases in waiting time, longer lines, tighter eligi-

> **The Missing Millionaires** Maryland increased the tax rate on million-dollar-a-year earners, and the number of such filers dropped from 3,000 in 2007 to 2,000 in 2008. Part of this result was due to the recession, but ample evidence also exists that tax rates affect economic behavior, as millionaires have the means to move their money to places where it earns the highest returns or engage in tax avoidance.[5]

bility requirements, rationing of services, and imposition of fees for service wherever possible. The good news is that using technology such as the Internet and other technologies to deliver government services may actually improve service levels in some cases.

However, cutbacks can have their own hidden costs and create turmoil. Early release of criminals from prison because the state can't afford the cost of incarceration and reductions in law enforcement budgets both present public safety issues. Outsourcing city services, such as garbage collection, will enrage the unions and lead to strikes and union-sponsored campaigns against public officials and groups that advocate such moves. Parks and other government properties may be closed or even sold to raise cash. Maintenance, testing, and inspection services may be reduced, creating public health hazards.

An unanticipated consequence for elected officials may be public refusal to accept such business as usual. This may appear as taxpayer revolts, protest marches, reform movements, or residents moving out of town, out of state, and even out of the country.

The Government Pension Time Bomb

Civil servants looking forward to a retirement with a pension, healthcare, and other benefits may experience a rude awakening. Between portfolio losses, reduced tax receipts, delayed funding due to the recession, and overly optimistic projections of returns on investments, the pension plans of twenty-one states were funded below 80 percent of their liabilities. The plans in Illinois and Kansas were only 54 and 60 percent funded, respectively, as of 2008. Due to the rough economy, more states have not been

> **The Trillion-Dollar Gap**
> The difference between the benefits states have promised their employees and what they actually have on hand to pay them amounts to $1 trillion, a shortfall of about 30 percent.[6]

making sufficient annual pension contributions to adequately fund their pension liabilities.[7]

While these promises to retirees may represent legally enforceable contracts, if the state doesn't have the money, it won't be able to pay out the benefits. It wouldn't be surprising to hear of some states (those in the worst shape) threatening bankruptcy when negotiating reduced pension payouts.

Living with the Unintended Consequences

Power and money is shifting to the public sector from the private sector in a big way. The result is an increasingly politicized economy and a society reeling from the effects of the unintended consequences of such actions. The government's massive spending hasn't led to significant and sustainable economic growth as promised and is potentially inflationary if it continues over an extended period of time. The result will be an increased cost of living on top of the other financial burdens Americans are being forced to carry.

Cutbacks in government services place a disproportionate burden on the poor, the displaced, and the disabled. In addition, the population tends to become polarized between those groups in favor with the politicians in power and those who are out of favor. The stress of uncertain employment and business survival takes a toll.

Wars not given the attention, commitment, and treasure they demand tend to end badly, setting the stage for more war in later years. Political scapegoating and the compromising of property rights create economic uncertainty for investors, lenders, and executives, inhibiting investment and job creation. Millions of retirees are finding (or will find) that their retirement plans—whether Social Security, 401(k), or government or union pensions—are providing less than they had hoped, and this results in profound implications for economic assumptions over the coming decade. Such are the unintended consequences of excessive spending and borrowing, compounded by inept political leadership.

PREDICTIONS	
Event	*Probability*
Another financial crisis will occur within ten years, and will be as bad—or worse—than the meltdown of 2008–09.	75%
Gold will reach unprecedented price levels: over $1,500/ounce.	75%
Credit will remain more expensive and less available, except for larger borrowers with near-perfect credit ratings and plenty of cash. Those who are politically connected will have access to financing with favorable terms.	80%
Total taxes, fees, and other government levies will rise to nearly half (or more) of the income of an individual with earnings above the national median average income.	85%

America's Spending Binge:
Winning Strategies for Us, as a Nation

The premise of this chapter is to warn of the potential unintended consequences if America continues to spend itself into a corner. However, the U.S. has seen even darker days before. Leadership matters, and tomorrow always has promise of a better day if the right decisions are made and executed effectively.

The good news is that we *can* recover if governments at all levels rein in excessive spending and reinvent themselves; if federal, state, and local governments steer away from trying to control the economy and stop pretending they can solve everyone's problems; and if the trend toward repeating the mistakes of the Great Depression (tight money, higher taxes, trade protectionism, over-regulation, and a political environment that inspires uncertainty rather than confidence) are reversed. The era of consumers, businesses, and governments living large by spending and borrowing has come to an end. All will need to start living within their means, and that is not necessarily a bad thing . . . once the pain of the de-leveraging hangover subsides.

America's Spending Binge: Winning Strategies for You, as a Leader

High unemployment in a difficult economy can present unintended consequences for employers. Downsizing can result in the loss of personnel with specialized knowledge that may not return when business recovers and your organization starts to rehire and grow again. While it will be possible to acquire talent at reasonable salaries, resist the temptation to treat your workforce as a faceless commodity. The companies that acquire talent strategically and empower their workforces to drive the business will gain a competitive edge.

Companies with manageable debt and predictable cash flow should have access to credit, but not as much nor as cheaply as in the past decade. Strategic acquisition of assets and resources at relatively low prices on favorable terms should pay off down the road.

Higher rates of taxation and regulation will negatively impact small, entrepreneurial businesses, the primary engine of job growth in the U.S. economy. New startups usually have the least resources to deal with a high level of regulation and taxation. Even larger businesses will be forced to raise prices to absorb these extra costs or face pressure on their profit margins and cash flow to service debt. Don't wait until the last minute to obtain permits or other services from a government agency. You can expect longer waits and higher fees.

America's Spending Binge:
Winning Strategies for You, Personally

You're going to feel it in the pocketbook in the foreseeable future, if you aren't already. According to research results reported in the *Chartist*, an investment newsletter, "On average, banking crises tend to last about seven years from beginning to end . . . government debt also surges by nearly 90 percent. Housing prices fall for around five years, with an average 36 percent decline, while stock prices tend to drop 56 percent with the decline lasting about three years."[8]

Successful businesses try to strengthen their financial position when faced with uncertainty and adversity, and you should do the same. Consider saving enough to cover living expenses for an extended period of time, such as six months or even a year.

Engage in personal development training activities to ensure that you are not only re-creating yourself for your current job, but also preparing for the next one. Such development efforts aren't limited to education either. Volunteer for additional roles in your organization to broaden your learning through on-the-job experience.

A trend can't be reversed overnight, especially one of this magnitude. We're in the midst of suffering from the Law of Unexpected Consequences. There will be success stories and recoveries alike, but at some point over the next decade, a climax in the de-leveraging of America will occur. Diversify your investments, maintain financial liquidity, and increase your earnings power by acquiring more skills and honing your talent.

Trend 7

Prices Gone Wild

Inflation Is Back, and So Is Deflation. Huh?

Close your eyes and picture trillions of dollars rolling off print-ing presses and being transported to a beach, where they are placed in helicopters and dropped out of the sky. Indeed, cen-tral banks in the U.S. and other industrialized countries have furiously printed money to arm their governments against the enemy Industrial Age politicians fear most: namely, the dread-ed economic phenomenon called *deflation*.

The collapse of the Industrial Age, like a glacial avalanche into the Arctic Ocean, is creating a global tidal wave of defla-tion. That tidal wave is picking up size and strength as it moves ominously toward our shores. The cause? Global markets are reacting to a glut of products and factories around the world, resulting in a gargantuan surplus of goods as a consequence of excesses from the Industrial Age. There are simply too many auto factories, retail stores, and McMansions when compared to current market demand.

Promoters and politicians worked together to seek, finance, and build excess manufacturing and other production capacity because they could not accept the idea of a new post-Industrial Global Innovation Age rendering obsolete their positions of privilege in the status quo of the Industrial Age.

Now, central bankers are moving with firm resolve, constructing financial breakwaters and reinforcing monetary bulwarks with freshly printed cash. Still, the bankers worry, "Will the deflationary waves wash away our economic models based on the hallowed premise that governments can wave a wand and create money out of thin air (also known as fiat money, or paper money, whereby money is not backed by gold or silver and whose face value is whatever the government says it is) and override market forces?"

We are witnessing an epic struggle between the forces of inflation and deflation. On the beach below those helicopters are the central bankers of the industrialized world. They have inflated and debased their currencies over the years to prop up the political expediency and overspending of their governments. Heading toward the beach is a tsunami of deflationary forces as the world wobbles under the burden of excess production capacity.

And this storm will not merely consist of just one huge tidal wave. Multiple storm waves will hit different areas of the economy in an unpredictable manner. Generalizations will not suffice to describe the storm effects and the damage inflicted.

Some asset categories and economic sectors will see asset values washed away, while others will survive and even rise in value.

Consequently, businesses, government agencies, nonprofits, and individuals will find forecasting their financial futures extraordinarily difficult. Imagine trying to develop a retirement plan using projections of inflation, spending, savings, and income, knowing those projections may have nothing to do with the reality coming.

> The U.S. Bureau of Labor Statistics provides an "Inflation Calculator" for measuring the decline of the dollar's purchasing power for time periods of your choosing. Check it out at bls.gov/data/inflation_calculator.htm. or go to www.jenkinsusa.com, which provides a link to the Inflation Calculator, along with other data and commentary on inflation and deflation.

You may be thinking, "What are you talking about? Isn't it an objective of the Federal Reserve Bank (the Fed) to control inflation?"

Just look at the facts. Since 1913, when the Federal Reserve Bank was created and placed in control of the U.S. currency, the value of a dollar has dropped over 95 percent.[2] In a more recent example, during Alan Greenspan's eighteen-year term as Chairman of the Federal Reserve Bank (from 1987 to 2006), the value of your paycheck fell by about half.[3] Yet Greenspan is considered by many to be one of the greatest central bankers of all time.

The Federal Reserve Bank's history reflects the precept that the economy can be "managed." Unfortunately, even the so-called "best and brightest" humans make awful mistakes. In 1929, the able chairman of the Federal Reserve Bank, Benjamin Strong, died. Leaderless, the Fed kept money tight long after the country slid into recession and allowed bankers to use low-cost funds borrowed from the Fed to fund speculators, at handsome profits, in an attempt to stimulate the economy. The resulting financial bubble collapsed into an economic meltdown.[4] In 2008, the Federal Reserve Bank, despite the failure of investment bank

Bear Stearns, incredibly, stood by and allowed Lehman Brothers to go bankrupt, along with its worldwide investment banking network. What had been a financial crisis quickly escalated into financial panic.

Who will win? Will it be inflation or deflation? If the central bankers of the West do everything just right, the big nations around the world cooperate, and no unexpected crises show up, the world could land on its monetary feet, but not without suffering a tumultuous period of price volatility and a lot of casualties along the way. If the politicians panic and force their central bankers to turn the presses on full speed, America and other overextended nations could face devastating hyperinflation. If the central bankers slow down the printing presses too much in an effort to preserve the value of the U.S. dollar (as our foreign creditors are demanding), deflation could wipe out asset valuations. We can only monitor events and the financial actions taken by the government as they unfold and react based on the likely consequences of the actions taken.

A Little Background, Please

Discussion of this trend should include definitions of inflation and deflation. *Inflation* is "a general increase in prices and fall in the purchasing value of money."[5] On the other hand, *deflation* is a "reduction of the general level of prices in an economy."[6]

Both inflation and deflation are based on the law of supply and demand. Money is a commodity. If the supply of money rises as the government printing presses speed up, its value tends to drop. When this happens, money buys less, reflecting inflation. When money supply is too tight, the economy slows, and the dollar buys more, reflecting deflation.

Factors other than money supply can affect the general level of prices for specific goods, services, and wages. When the major oil-producing countries formed a cartel to control prices of their major export in 1973, oil prices spiked as these countries reined in supplies.

A major key commodity used in a wide range of products exhibits a rippling effect as inflation or deflation takes hold. A good example of the rippling effect, in terms of inflation, is an uptick in oil prices. As energy prices rise, the impact is felt across the board. Food costs more, travel costs more, and the overall price tag for living increases; inflation is taking hold.

Momentum is another effect. As prices rise or fall, the impact leads to an acceleration of the trend. The decline of the housing market, which started in 2006, is an example of the momentum effect. As home values plummeted, homeowners suddenly found themselves without enough equity to refinance their home loans. Many of these people held adjustable rate mortgages, with interest rates that were about to adjust upward. With their homes deflated of value, they could not qualify for a new mortgage, and many homeowners could not afford the price tag of their adjusted interest rates. Foreclosures ran rampant, further depressing home valuations.

A role of the Federal Reserve Bank is to mitigate the effects of these two economic trends. If inflation begins to increase beyond an acceptable range, the Fed raises interest rates to stem the money supply. If deflation is causing the economy to stall, it will lower interest rates to make money more accessible.

So, what happens when these two economic forces strike at the same time? What happens when misguided government policies lead to inflation, while market forces trigger deflation? Unfortunately, we know all too well what happens because that's our current plight, and it's one of the reasons why this is a trend you can't ignore.

Rolling Inflation and Deflation

A general rise or fall in prices associated with inflation or deflation may apply only to a specific type of goods, location, or economic sector and not the broad economy. A suitable term for this is "rolling" inflation or deflation. Two examples are:

> ➤ During the 1980s, recession rolled through various regions of the U.S. while other regions were growing.
> ➤ Oil prices may rise while lumber prices fall.

Such spikes and downdrafts may last months or even years. Forecasters who only focus on the big (macro) picture miss the impact of inflation or deflation affecting specific assets, commodities, regions, and sectors.

A Profile of the Forces of Inflation

The rallying cry from our nation's capital has always been to keep tabs on inflation. Without a doubt, inflation can wreak havoc on an economy, and our government is always ready to roll out its watchdogs to scapegoat others when inflation becomes problematic.

Unfortunately, when the government uses its control of the money supply to solve problems such as a credit crisis, inflation can result. According to Gary Wolfram, PhD, of the Business & Media Institute, "Some economists . . . recognized some time ago that the Federal Reserve was increasing the amount of money as a mechanism to solve the credit crisis, which was, to a certain extent, caused by prior Fed policy, and warned that we would be seeing a rise in inflation as a result."[7]

Beyond the Federal Reserve, however, the government can initiate inflationary trends, particularly through policy. Here are some examples:

Energy: The government has long dragged its feet on market-based energy programs that would relieve our dependence on oil and energy from foreign countries. Meanwhile, public officials have limited offshore drilling and new nuclear power plants. Every state has its own set of restrictions on building new refineries, and we haven't had a new oil refinery built on U.S. soil for producing gasoline in a quarter century. Meanwhile, the pursuit of alternative fuels has an erratic history, and some that have been focused on, like the inefficient non-solution known as ethanol, have amounted to little more than subsidies.

Food: The U.S. government's support of ethanol development caused farmers to convert their wheat crops to corn. As a result, we were faced with a dramatic decrease in wheat production, leading to higher prices. In the end, we wound up with an alternative fuel that is both inefficient and insufficient—not to mention higher food prices because of the wheat shortage.

Healthcare: The government has made promises to expand heath insurance coverage, but we already have a chronic shortage of doctors and nurses. To recruit and retain these professionals will cost more, not less.

Education: As public colleges and universities sought higher levels of funding, more federal and state dollars were pumped into the institutions. This resulted in tuition increases and larger student loans to pay. As state budgets tighten and student loan terms and conditions become more stringent, deflation can take hold on university budgets.

On the elementary and secondary levels, our tax dollars continue to feed a public school system heavy on bureaucracy, but too often light on results. Legions of dedicated, competent teaching professionals toil within the system, but the institutional mindset has been unable to generate productivity increases to offset rising costs. It costs us more money than ever before to produce a populace too often not adequately prepared for the demands of the new economy and unprepared to win in the Global Innovation Age.

Bureaucracy: Massive government bureaucracy doesn't come cheap. The state and federal governments include incredible pension liabilities. Ask anyone, and they will probably agree that a government job generally includes better benefits relative to the private sector. These great benefits and pension programs are costly, and in bad times, governments have traditionally raised taxes or borrowed more money to pay for these programs instead of passing along the pain. These benefit programs will change as the cost of the benefits, along with other entitlement programs, strain the ability of state and local governments (who can't simply print more money like the Feds) to raise the cash to cover the costs.

Regulation and Taxes: The government will assure you that regulations help everyone play by the rules, but that sense of order comes at a price. Consider housing, for example. Government bodies establish restrictions on zoning, how much land can be developed, how homes are to be constructed, and other facets of real estate, limiting and narrowing options and driving up the overall cost . . . and prices.

Taxes also add to the costs. Need proof? Take a look at the additional taxes levied on your airplane tickets. All the post–9/11 protection costs money, and you feel the inflation every time you buy a ticket.

And in This Corner, the Forces of Deflation

Deflation scares the daylights out of politicians and businesses, but only if it occurs at the wrong time and for the wrong reason. If productivity gains cause an increase in supply without an increase in cost, this leads to an increase in wealth. People can buy more things for less money: Think DVD players, big-screen TVs, and personal computers, for instance.

However, if the opposite occurs and wages and credit decrease while other items increase in cost, the effect can be very bad. "If deflation is caused by a decreasing supply of money, as in the Great Depression, that would not be good. The stock market crash sucked all the liquidity out of the marketplace, the economy contracted, people lost their jobs, and then banks stopped loaning money because people were defaulting. The problem compounded as more people lost their jobs, and money supply fell further, causing more people to lose their jobs, etc., etc."[8]

Game Changers

A number of marketplace trends are taking place that are threatening the government's money game of moderate inflation to keep the economy moving along and the voters relatively passive. Among them:

Commoditization: As we achieve remarkable new advances in technology and manufacturing, the price tag for products can dip to commodity levels. The advance of the semiconductor chip has led to exponentially lower costs for electronics. Innovation is occurring at an accelerated pace, so the added value that differentiates products and services from others becomes obsolete or minimized at a much faster pace than before.

Outsourcing opportunities in India and China have also contributed to dramatic declines in production costs. In terms of quality and features, the difference between a low-priced import versus a higher-priced domestically produced item in terms of utility may simply not be great enough to justify a large price disparity.

Panic: When deflation continues to take hold, people tend to refrain from buying more. It's the dreaded deflationary spiral; consumers try to get by on less and seek that which costs the least amount of money and still covers their basic needs. It directly contravenes the stimulus programs the government initiates in the hope to jumpstart the economy.

Shrinking wages: The outsourcing of blue- and white-collar jobs has led to deflationary effects on wages. Outsourcing has caused many corporations to limit pay raises for many white-collar workers. In the post-Industrial Age, the ranks of union factory jobs have been decimated. For blue-collar workers, the deflationary impact has been devastating: An unskilled worker now typically

(Continued)

> *(Continued)*
>
> makes ten to twelve dollars an hour with limited benefits instead of thirty to forty dollars an hour (or more) with benefits, as was common in the Industrial Age union shops.
>
> **Inventory:** Businesses can adjust and manage inventory they have on hand. It may require some write-downs and fire sales, but most excess inventory can be disposed of one way or another. Production capacity is far more difficult, expensive, and time consuming to deal with. Question: What do you do with a factory operating well below capacity or a distribution center no one wants or needs? Answer: Keep paying for it! Closing a plant or facility is extremely expensive, maybe more than the business can afford.

Sound familiar? Yes. Sound scary? YES. Deflation also exposes financial "smoke and mirrors" (e.g., Bernie Madoff) and requires politically unpopular decisions. Inflation, on the other hand, covers up a lot of poorly conceived spending by allowing debt to be paid with inflated dollars and gives the illusion that incomes and asset values are rising.

Shortages in the Land of Plenty

In 2010, with a still-tepid economy, bottlenecks and shortages showed up in company supply chains. From machine tools to electronic components, purchasing agents and suppliers reported delivery delays that resulted in lost orders. The recession forced many suppliers out of business, many workers to be laid off, and inventory stocks to be lowered. As businesses recovered, the supply lines could not react fast enough to handle the higher volume to prevent disruptions in supplies.

Over time, such disruptions would normally be expected to work themselves out. However, in an unstable economy with rolling deflation and inflation, inadequate supplies will continue to be a problem as businesses experience greater difficulty in forecasting demand; and the pressure will be on to minimize inventories and overhead.

In regard to other resources, potential shortages have been delayed, though not eliminated, by the severe economic downturn of 2008–09. The U.S. electrical grid was only a few years away from shortages of electricity when the recession hit. However, the problem of a lack of new generation hasn't been resolved. Windmills and solar power will not be able to fill in the potential gaps of availability in five to ten years, due to problems involved with having the electricity when needed and adequate energy distribution networks. "The transmission-line shortage is threatening to slow wind energy's breakneck growth and could prevent some states from meeting renewable energy mandates," explains SmartGridNews.com.[9]

Beyond delivery delays, a greater underlying force is at work moving the U.S. toward scarcity. Ever more strategic natural resources, such as oil, minerals, and metals, are being gobbled up by other nations who are in competition with, or hostile, to American interests. During the Great Recession of 2008–09, for instance, Chinese companies took advantage of de-pressed prices to purchase tens of billions of essential natural resource assets around the world.[10]

Oil prices have surged since the bottom of the 2008–09 re-cession. The Gulf oil spill and concurrent moratorium on off-shore drilling in that region has aggravated the oil availability. But oil itself is only part of the problem. As mentioned earlier in this chapter, growth of oil refining capacity in the U.S. has been limited. So, even if the oil is available, a bottleneck exists for converting this resource into useable products, like gasoline.

Water is becoming a resource with the potential for regional shortages in the western portion of the U.S. Those regions with ample fresh water, such as the Great Lakes region, both on the American and the Canadian side, are not about to give away this precious resource.

Mining, timber, and other natural resources, along with oil and water, are becoming increasingly subject to conflict between the users, producers, and third party interest groups as all compete to direct such resources toward supporting their own agendas. The result can sometimes be tragic. California's San Joaquin Valley, a highly productive agricultural region dependent on irrigation systems, experienced an economic disaster in 2009 when the federal government shut off the valley's water supplies and redirected those waters to protect an endangered fish species, the delta smelt.[11]

The trend toward scarcity is inherently inflationary, but given a rollercoaster global economy, demand and supply can vacillate significantly year to year by various types of supplies and assets, which, in turn, creates rolling inflation and deflation.

Déjà Vu

The problems of inflation and deflation are nothing new to the U.S. The term "worthless as a Continental" referred to the inflation-ravaged money the Continental Congress issued during the Revolutionary War (Yes, America had a Congress before the country achieved independence, and the political gamesmanship played then was every bit as frustrating and agenda-driven as it is now).

Yet the young country paid back its bonds at full face value under the leadership of Alexander Hamilton, while he was a member of Washington's cabinet. There is a reason the U.S. Constitution called for U.S. currency to be backed by silver and other specie, like gold, rather than allowing money to be printed as dictated by government officials. Americans had already learned the hard way in the aftermath of the American Revolution to limit what politicians could do with the money supply. Nevertheless, the U.S. abandoned silver coinage in 1965 and the gold standard in 1971.

We're experiencing an economic dilemma, and there is no easy way out. As politically inspired inflation continues to climb, the invisible hand of the marketplace counters with deflationary forces. And because we are leveraging ourselves to the hilt on both a macro and micro level, there's little reserve to absorb shocks to the financial system.

PREDICTIONS	
Event	*Probability*
Inflation and deflation will be a rollercoaster ride—not just generally, but by types of assets, products, and services as well.	85%
The purchasing power of the U.S. dollar will be less within five years, compared to the value of the dollar on January 1, 2010.	99%

Prices Gone Wild: Winning Strategies for Us, as a Nation

The possibility exists that political policies may slip out of control and produce unexpected consequences such as severe inflation or deflation. Crosscurrents of inflation and deflation can roll through various assets, regions, and sectors. When deflationary forces come to the forefront, expect the Federal Reserve Bank to try everything possible to re-inflate. But no matter what they try to do, the market's recessionary and deflationary forces may be too powerful to hold back.

What can we do? Energy is at the top of the list, and it will probably require a wholesale solution. We need to increase our refinery capacity, homogenize our state standards regarding gasoline, and eliminate programs like the ethanol agenda that carry unintended consequences like price increases in commodity items like wheat.

We also need to be extremely wary of political upheaval. High inflation and economic depression can open the door for powerful demagogues. Hitler began his rise to power in the aftermath of Germany's hyper-inflation of 1923. Huey Long tried to seize control of Louisiana and possessed national ambitions during the deflationary Great Depression. Whether the problem is severe inflation or deflation, we face inherent risks that we must guard against.

Most of all, we need to be cautious of increased interest rates, higher taxes, more trade restrictions, and greater regulation. If the government moves us further in this direction, deflation could overrun all attempts to turn it back.

When the economy is not doing well, consumers can negotiate lower prices for services; and during deflationary periods, prices for domestically produced goods can drop in the face of reduced demand. However, when the U.S. dollar falls in value, the cost of imports like oil will rise regardless of whether the economy is doing poorly or well.

Prices Gone Wild: Winning Strategies for You, as a Leader

You're navigating through turbulent times. The rule of thumb is to be ready for either inflation or deflation. The likelihood of long-term price stability is unlikely; trends will be erratic. Arm yourself with a Plan A, and a Plan B, and assume you may need to abandon one in a heartbeat to pick up the other.

More than ever before, adhere to principles like just-in-time manufacturing. Excess inventory could be a deathblow during these uncertain times, with two exceptions: 1) your fastest-turning items and 2) critical parts that you simply can't afford to have out of stock. Increase your inventory turns, and establish as direct a relationship with vendors as possible.

Tread lightly around long-term fixed-price contracts. If you lock into a long-term contract at a deflated price, it could be a good thing for business. On the other hand, if prices drop even further, you could wind up eating the difference. As a rule of thumb, make sure you have an exit strategy under a variety of scenarios. Stay nimble, and keep a close eye on the markets.

Prices Gone Wild: Winning Strategies for You, Personally

During deflationary times, debt is your worst enemy. Pay off as much of your debt as possible and stay liquid. Reducing your debt load during these tough times is essential: In an uncertain economy, your job status is always uncertain.

Diversify your assets so that neither inflation nor deflation will wipe you out. During the transition from the Industrial Age to the Global Innovation Age, there will be periods so tumultuous that investment success for many may well be defined as "He/she who loses the least wins." In such periods, survival and preservation of your money will be paramount.

Trend 8

The Demographic Time Bomb

Will the Economy Survive the Explosion?

Political debate has swirled over the construction of a wall along the Mexican/U.S. border. Advocates believe constructing an expansive, impenetrable wall is the only way to quell the influx of illegal aliens. It worked with King Kong, right?

Putting aside the question of the "rightness" or "wrongness" of erecting a wall between two neighboring countries with intertwined economies and cultures, the rationale of such a wall is rather short-sighted. In the coming years, we may have walls along the U.S. borders, but it won't be to prevent people from entering our country. Those walls will be there to keep American citizens from leaving. After all, a mass exodus is a possibility, and its cause is the Demographic Time Bomb that is ticking at this very moment. That bomb refers to the retiring Baby Boomer population.

According to the U.S. Census Bureau, there are approximately 78.2 million Baby Boomers, and they represent nearly

30 percent of the U.S. population. The oldest Boomers, born between 1946 and 1964, will begin turning sixty-five in the year 2011. In a little over twenty years, the number of Americans sixty-five or older will double.[1] Their impending retirement will have a tremendous impact on the country's infrastructure, including Medicare, Social Security, our overall health system, and our workforce.

The Demographic Time Bomb will present a serious challenge to this country. It's inevitable—a trend you absolutely can't ignore. In eight years, our nation's citizens could face limited income opportunities, declining health services, and a drop in living standards. Better build the wall, Washington D.C., and you had better build it fast!

The Demographic Time Bomb: The Trend

The Baby Boomers represent the generation born following World War II, when America launched into a period of sustained growth. In the post-war years, U.S. manufacturing infrastructure was intact, and America enjoyed unequaled prosperity by supplying European and Asian countries recovering from wartime destruction. As our living spaces expanded into the suburbs, so did our population, and the Baby Boomer generation took hold.

The good life also gave birth to a new sense of social activism. As the Baby Boomers blossomed, their attitudes toward the prosperous society before them became part of the social fabric. Following the "Greatest Generation," in which sacrifice was the norm, the Boomers came to expect the good life that had been bestowed upon them. High-paying jobs, easily accessible healthcare service, and home ownership became entitlements.

Walls Along the Border
. . . we may have walls along America's borders. . . . Those walls will be there to keep American citizens from leaving.

This sense of social activism grew as the Boomers aged. As their fellow Boomers took political office, their beliefs translated into bulging government budgets and increasing amounts of debt. Every social problem became everyone's problem, and our tax dollars were spent (wisely or unwisely, depending on your perspective) on ever-expanding safety nets.

Now that the Boomers have expanded the infrastructure of social programs, what will happen when they begin to draw from it during their retirement years? In the past, our population had a more balanced ratio of retirees to taxpayers, like a seesaw on which both sides held equal weight. With the Boomers retiring, though, one side of the seesaw will inevitably be overloaded, and the taxpayers will literally be left high and dry. According to the U.S. Census Bureau, in 2006 there were 3.3 workers for every 1 Social Security beneficiary. In 2031, when all the Baby Boomers are over sixty-five, the ratio will be 2.1 to 1.[2]

Here's an overview of the shock waves the Demographic Time Bomb will send through our society.

The Social Security (Dis)Trust

Back in 1935, when Social Security was created, the American public was promised that the payroll taxes paid into the system would be placed in a trust and used only to pay out Social Security benefits. That changed in 1969, as Congress couldn't resist tapping such a large pot of money to help pay for the Vietnam War and Great Society programs.

All of those payroll taxes are now swept into the federal government's general fund, where the money is used, in part, to pay for the pensions of government officials, national defense and bridges to nowhere, as well as the other expenditures authorized by Congress. All that remains of the Social Security Trust are file cabinets filled with IOUs. Members of Congress will reassure retirees that these IOUs are backed by the "full faith and credit" of the United States of America. The reality is that Social Security amounts to trillions of dollars of unfunded liabilities that will ultimately have to be funded and paid back with interest at some point. To pay for such borrowing would require an extraordinary level of taxation.

Back in 2005, Alan Greenspan, Chairman of the Federal Reserve Bank at the time, addressed the ability of the U.S. government to pay back those IOUs to fund Social Security: "I fear that we may already have committed more physical resources to the baby-boom generation in its retirement years than our economy has the capacity to deliver."[3]

According to David Walker, former Comptroller General of the United States and head of the General Accountability Office (GAO), "We face large and structural deficits largely due to known demographic trends and rising healthcare costs . . . Closing the current long-term fiscal gap based on reasonable assumptions would require real average annual economic growth in the double-digit range every year for the next seventy-five years. During the 1990s, the economy grew at an average 3.2 percent per year. As a result, we cannot simply grow our way out of this problem. Tough choices will be required."[4] It's a lose/lose situation.

The public, justifiably irate that they've been led into this quagmire, will be ready to revolt. The thought of throngs of Boomers marching on Washington D.C. is not hard to imagine, as Washington has seen its share of marches in the past. How will the government react to this march though? It will take real courage for politicians to clean up the mess, and even if they have what it takes, there's no assurance the public will continue to tolerate or trust their public officials.

Healthcare

Besides overburdening the nation's tax base, the Boomers' demand for healthcare will far exceed the supply. According to a 2008 report from the Institutes of Medicine (IOM), "The nation faces an impending healthcare crisis as the number of older patients with more complex health needs increasingly outpaces the number of healthcare providers with the knowledge and skills to adequately care for them."[5] This doesn't bode well for a healthcare system that is already currently experiencing shortages of nurses and doctors.

The Sickest Generation

> Americans in their mid-fifities (Baby Boomers) reported themselves to be in poorer health and in more pain than the previous generation approaching retirement.—National Bureau of Economic Research
> Four out of five adults over the age of fifty have at least one chronic condition. Eleven million live with five or more chronic conditions.—AARP Study
> One out of eight Boomers will suffer Alzheimer's disease.—Fisher Center for Alzheimer's Research Foundation
> Osteoarthritis is a common condition among older Baby Boomers.—*Nutritional Outlook*
> A study reported that half of the oldest Baby Boomers have high blood pressure and two in five are obese.—Centers for Disease Control and Prevention

The U.S. Bureau of Labor Statistics notes that our annual expenditures on healthcare will undoubtedly rise. Expenditures in 2004 averaged $2,695 for people ages forty-five to fifty-four, a group comprised primarily of Baby Boomers. Imagine the impact on healthcare costs when these people hit the ages of fifty-five to sixty-four and the cost per person jumps to $3,262; and then sixty-five and over, when the costs are at $3,899 per person (not adjusted for inflation).[6]

An increasingly aging population, coupled with severe shortages in the healthcare workforce, could lead to lower quality medical services in some cases. The horrific stories you read occasionally about patients dying from improper care in hospitals may become more commonplace.

Besides medical care, long-term care in the form of assisted living and nursing homes will reach crisis proportions. Currently, Medicaid reimbursement rates are below cost. Faced with an assured money-losing proposition, long-term care facilities have been cutting back or abandoning the market for low-income seniors. The result is a declining supply of long-term care resources for Medicaid patients. Meanwhile, demand will grow dramatically over the next two decades.

This is particularly bad news for Baby Boomers, especially considering the expectation of ever-increasing life spans. Not only will the Boomer generation have to struggle with their long-term care needs, but many will also be responsible for the care of their aging parents—yet another strain on an already over-burdened healthcare system.

Retirement Prospects for the Baby Boomers

The Congressional Budget Office summed up the prospects for the Boomer generation as ". . . about a quarter of Baby Boomer households have so far failed to accumulate significant savings. They appear likely to depend entirely on government benefits in retirement. At the other end of the spectrum, at least half of the households are expected to maintain their working-age standard of living during retirement (*under the assumption that current laws governing federal benefit programs do not change*) [Ed., italics added]. For the remaining quarter of Boomer households, the evidence is mixed: under midrange assumptions about saving, rates of return, and retirement age, they appear set to experience moderate declines in their living standard during retirement, which could be offset by modestly increasing saving and by working for a few more years."[7]

The Stock Market and Real Estate

If you think the volatility of *today's* stock and real estate markets has been hard to take, buckle your seatbelts. The Baby Boomers will also cause seismic shifts in two time-honored, moneymaking investments: stocks and real estate.

For the stock market, the biggest downside will be the loss of capital. Baby Boomers will be cashing in their investments to pay for their retirement, draining money from their investment accounts rather than contributing more money. Reduced money flows to retirement accounts will affect the availability of capital for overall economic growth. Wharton finance professor Jeremy Siegel calls the impending retirement trend "the granddaddy of all demographic shifts." He warns that stocks and other assets could plunge by as much as 50 percent.[8] However, such a plunge is not inevitable, and the reductions in retirement account contributions could be offset by inflows of other sources of capital, provided pro-growth economic government policies are pursued.

The real estate market will struggle in a similar fashion. Almost four out of five (78 percent) Boomer households are homeowners, and one in four Boomers owns other real estate in addition to a primary residence.[9] Many Boomers have considered the equity in their home to be their main source of retirement funding. Whenever their home values tumble, as they did following the subprime debacle starting in 2006, these Boomers will find their retirement nest egg smaller than anticipated. But there is an exception to the above expectation: Any return of significant inflation should boost the value of well-located and attractive properties.

Workforce

The workforce will also change as the Baby Boomers begin to retire. Nationally, half the current workforce will be eligible to retire in the next decade—half! With so many people leaving the full-time workforce, the available talent pool for positions requiring considerable talent and experience will dwindle. The Boomers possess years of experience and expertise, and there won't be enough skilled people left in the following generations to replace those skills. Consequently, we can expect significant numbers of Boomers to remain in the workforce full-time, as well as part-time or on an interim basis, even beyond usual retirement age. They will be essential for knowledge transfers, mentoring, and specialized skills.

Fortunately (or unfortunately, depending on your perspective), many of the Boomers simply won't be able to retire. As eligibility for social programs tightens and healthcare grows more expensive, retirees' fixed incomes won't be able to pick up the slack. Many seniors will return to the workforce. They'll work part-time, on an interim basis, or as independent contractors, in addition to seeking full-time employment.

By this point, you should understand why the Demographic Time Bomb is one of the most important trends changing the economy. These changes are inevitable, even though they will not occur overnight. The real impact of the bomb will start to be felt around the time period of 2016 to 2020, when the number of Boomers having reached retirement age becomes significant in terms of the total population.

That gives us time, but that small window of opportunity may be of little use. We may not have the political willpower or the foresight to move this country into the bunkers before the Time Bomb goes *BOOM!*

Back to that Wall Along the Border

The possibility of a wall constructed along America's border to keep people *in* the country, not out of it, was discussed at the beginning of this chapter. Specifically, a growing number of senior citizens can be expected to head out of the U.S. in search of less expensive healthcare and living costs, as well as a more comfortable lifestyles. Expatriate communities to the south of the U.S. are likely to grow from the Boomer migration. In particular, nations like Panama and Belize, where English, legal rights, and acceptance of the U.S. dollar are woven into the economic fabric, should experience heightened interest from U.S. residents.

PREDICTIONS	
Event	*Probability*
The eligibility age for Social Security retirement benefits will be increased, and benefits will be reduced for higher earners and/or workers under the age of fifty-five.	80%
Inflation will diminish the value of Social Security benefits, regardless of any cost-of-living adjustments in the program.	90%
Long-term care for Baby Boomers, especially low-income seniors, will become a crisis within a decade, give or take a few years.	85%

The Demographic Time Bomb:
Winning Strategies for Us, as a Nation

Use whatever analogy you want. Call the looming Baby Boomer transition to retirement a ticking time bomb, a hole in the dike, or a dam ready to burst. No matter what you call it, this trend is going to place demands on society that America is unprepared to effectively deal with. There is no time left to "do something" that's painless. The *something* that will be done will translate into reduced benefits and a leaner lifestyle than currently anticipated by many Baby Boomers, if not most of them.

We can overcome these problems, but it will take strict financial discipline and a reinvention of American politics, the U.S. workforce, and a sense-of-entitlement culture. We're going to trudge through some tough times.

The Demographic Time Bomb:
Winning Strategies for You, as a Leader

First, consider taking a multi-generational view to your work-force with each generation bringing along its special needs, wants, and attitudes. You can expect a lot of Boomer consultants and part-time workers to pepper your ranks, many of them looking for benefits and a source of income to offset their reduced government benefits. Your workforce, young or old, will need to be more productive than ever, particularly with profit margins dwindling. Talent will matter more than ever before, but small companies may have a much more difficult time competing against the big corporations for the top guns.

Your healthcare costs and structure will obviously change, though what healthcare insurance coverage will look like ten years down the road is impossible to predict, even in a book full of predictions. Your physical workplace will also be altered. Either you'll have to retrofit your accommodations to handle more people with disabilities, or you'll convert to a virtual workplace so people can be productive from the comfort of their own homes.

No matter what business you're in, you can expect the free-spending Baby Boomers to do an abrupt about face. They will morph into a generation generally described as penny pinchers. Consider converting your product to offer a more value-based model (if this scenario seems implausible, consider how the "flower child" generation of the 1970s evolved into the "yuppies" of the '80s).

The predominant survival model will be that of nimble organizations that sell products and services viable in international markets. With the U.S. consumer marketplace in a mature state, developing economies will be the hotbed of new consumerism. If you can't sell outside America's borders, you're going to have a tough time growing.

The Demographic Time Bomb:
Winning Strategies for You, Personally

On working: How you navigate through this potentially rocky time will depend on your understanding of market needs and your skill set. If you're innovative, creative, and willing to adapt, you'll be sought after, but if you're content to "just get by," there may not be a place for you. Why? In a challenging economy, jobs will go to the most highly qualified. Taking calculated risks, with a contingency plan in place that will allow an affordable exit and avoid catastrophic consequences if the risk doesn't work out, will be an avenue to winning in the Global Innovation Age.

On investing: Homeownership still makes sense. Condominiums for retiring Boomers that offer accessibility features (i.e., wider doorways, few or no steps, and other ease-of-use features) along with enhanced security and street-level access to the unit are likely to be in high demand.

Dividend-paying stocks will make a big comeback, as Boomers seek income while waiting for capital appreciation. However, a "buy-and-hold" investment approach will probably not work as well as during the past fifty years, given the upheaval facing the markets. Timing will become a more important investment consideration.

Depressed real estate with cash flow that covers all financing costs, plus a 12+ percent return on investment, can present real opportunities. Speculative investments in vacant property can be even more rewarding, but it will be necessary to have a strong turnaround strategy in place before making the purchase.

On healthcare: Re-read "Trend 3: Healthcare on Life Support."

On not becoming a victim: Fraud and misrepresentation will become a growing problem as Boomers age. Seniors are prime targets of con artists seeking to exploit their frustrations.

Troubled sellers may try to take shortcuts at your expense, so a healthy dose of skepticism will be needed. Develop a circle of trusted advisors now.

Trend 9

The Knock Heard 'Round the World

Global Market Opportunities Are Knocking.
Who Will Let Them In?

The phrase "the shot heard 'round the world" has different meanings in different regions of the world. In the United States, it's associated with the start of the Revolutionary War. In Europe, it correlates with the assassination of Archduke Franz Ferdinand and the beginning of World War I. In Russia, a shot fired from the battle cruiser *Aurora* was heralded as the start of the Bolshevik Revolution.

Today, the shot has been replaced by a knock. Opportunity is knocking for businesses, and it's no longer confined to affluent countries. With the advent of the digital age and the flattening of the world through globalized communications, the world has become an open market. Opportunities can now happen anywhere in the world.

No bloodshed will follow the knock heard 'round the world (we hope), but it does carry the same revolutionary fervor as previous shots. Nations with infrastructure (such as manufac-

> "For thousands of years, trade routes were considered important to the regional sustainability of every civilization. Those trade routes are now electronic."—James Carlini[1]

turing plants and equipment) no longer have a lock on the world's wealth. You can make anything, anywhere, thanks to digital technology from the Internet to the Blackberry; distance has become virtually irrelevant, and computing is nearly free (with some qualification and a few limitations).[2]

As the world has grown more connected, the number of consumers eager for goods has increased. It is estimated that the number of people with disposable income available for consumer goods will triple by the end of this decade, to roughly three billion. That's a staggering number, but it doesn't necessarily mean that lines will be three times longer at your local-Walmart. This huge jump in the number of consumers means new opportunities will occur overseas, as well as in the "industrialized" countries, providing American companies a chance to tap into new markets.

Why is this so? The numbers tell the story. The U.S. is a market of approximately 300 million consumers. The European Union (all twenty-seven countries) about 500 million; Mexico, about 106 million; Brazil has a population of nearly 200 million; Indonesia and the Philippines in southeast Asia, with a combined population of 330 million, have slightly more than the U.S. population. Now, consider China and India as part of the global market, with just these two countries having a combined population of roughly two and a half billion people, over one-third of all the people on the face of the Earth.[3]

Companies in India Tap Low-Income Market

Even the poor represent a market opportunity in the Global Innovation Age. Indian firms are busy developing low cost products and services aimed at low income consumers. Examples include:

> A heart monitor redesigned to reduce its cost by 90 percent.
> Portable bank branches, costing $200 each, that keep overhead and fees low.
> A $70 battery-powered refrigerator.[4]

While a majority of the people in the still-developing nations may still be poor and eking out a subsistence living, middle and working classes with disposable income are growing. Still, the poor represent such a large market in developing nations that homegrown entrepreneurs are learning how to market to those with limited means. Consumerism is becoming a worldwide phenomenon. The opportunity to grow exponentially in a global market has arrived.

The successful businessperson understands that in this case, the proverbial glass is half full. Globalized marketing opportunities are all around us, providing a unique chance for businesses to seek and find new customers for their products. Opportunity is knocking in a big way, making this a very, very good trend—one that simply can't be ignored.

The "Giant Sucking Sound" No One Heard . . . Because it Didn't Happen

More trade can pay for a lot of costs at home. The increased business activity can offset tax increases and new regulatory burdens. Bill Clinton's administration is a case in point, with two contentious events occurring that proved fortuitous for his presidency. The first of these was adding Mexico to the North American Free Trade Agreement (NAFTA), in 1994. Championed by the president, it would expand the lines of trade between the United States, Canada, and Mexico. Trade unions, protectionists, and Ross Perot were up in arms, cautioning people to beware of the "giant sucking sound" from south of the border. Independent presidential candidate Ross Perot engaged in a spirited debate with Vice President Al Gore over the merits of NAFTA. Gore showed some debating dexterity, and Congress eventually settled on the premise that NAFTA would be a net gain. The passage of NAFTA did increase trade between the two countries. The resulting U.S. trade losses that took place were offset by a boost in new economic activity, (admittedly, some of the gains came at the expense of lower-skilled U.S. workers). The timing couldn't have been better for Clinton, because the second contentious event occurred at the same time—the largest tax increase in history (up to that time).

In 1993, Clinton had just pushed through the Omnibus Budget Reconciliation Act (OBRA-93). It was projected to "increase federal revenues by $241 billion between 1994 and 1998," according to the Congressional Budget Office.[5] Regardless of your political stance on taxation or how Clinton's tax boosts were allocated, there was no denying this large tax increase would take a bite out of Americans' wallets and impact the economy.

However, the economy did not falter. Clinton aggressively pursued trade agreements, including the expansion of the North American Free Trade Agreement (NAFTA) and the creation of the World Trade Organization (WTO). The resulting increase in trade offset the impact of the new tax burden. Growth of U.S. manufacturing output in the decade following NAFTA grew faster than in the prior decade, and trade between the three nations of NAFTA tripled between 1994 and 2008.[6]

What Goes Around Comes Around

A wide-open global economy means companies from foreign countries will be soliciting business on American shores to a greater extent. We will feel even more intense competition from overseas. As a result, while we're looking to expand elsewhere, we'll also be faced with defending our home turf.

Technology, Property Rights, a Global Language and Financial Fusion

What, specifically, has led to the rise of globalized market opportunities? A number of factors have contributed heavily to the ease with which international trade now takes place:

Technology First

Communication used to present a problem for businesses. Communication and interaction with foreign companies used to be extremely difficult due in great part to geographic hurdles. Today's "snail mail" seems like the Pony Express of the 1800s.

The rise of the Internet at the turn of the century changed everything. The massive buildup of technological infrastructure, fueled by technology speculators, enabled high-speed communications to take place on a global scale. Nowadays, it's possible to conduct numerous working relationships, all from one central location.

For example, a construction company can monitor and manage several job sites from one central location. Photographs and videos can be taken and digitally transmitted, and cell phone communication and email allow for specific instructions to be relayed back to the worksite.

English as First Language

Another major hindrance to communication was the formidable language barrier, which lent itself to complications from production to marketing. In a fortuitous development for the United States, English has become the predominant language of business throughout the world. "The Internet and the popularity of American movies contribute to English-language dominance," said Gary Waissai, Dean of the Arizona State University's School of Global Management and Leadership.[7] His colleague, Mike Seiden, President of Western International University, also notes that "emerging markets such as India and China do much of their business in English."[8]

Business Interests Backed by Law

On an international basis, contract, intellectual property, and trade laws are becoming stronger. This is a major development in emerging countries, where copycat manufacturers routinely bypass patents and intellectual property.

Thomas Friedman noted this behavioral change on the part of India. "There is no question we did want India to have intellectual

(Continued)

(Continued)
property protection to protect our products. But what turned out
was that a lot of Indians wanted it as well because they became innovators themselves."[9] By making the playing field fair, the game
has taken on a new dimension, and it will continue to improve as
countries become more sophisticated.

The Decline in Currency Exchange Restrictions
The Euro and the European Common Market have contributed significantly to reducing currency restrictions. As money flows freely,
trade becomes easier.

Dealing with different currencies is what helped London dis-
place New York as the world's financial center. "The main factor
was the willingness of banks in London to use other countries' currency when [British] sterling was no longer sought after. Dollars
came first, then the Deutschmark and yen. . . ." wrote Anthony Hilton on the financial website "This is Money."[10]

What about cheap foreign labor taking our jobs? And low-
cost imports flooding our markets while our factories are forced
to close? Not to mention the environmental damage poisoning the
Earth in China and elsewhere. Don't forget about the trade barriers Japan, China, and other countries have put in place to protect
their domestic businesses. And, in an age of knowledge, shouldn't
China be required to respect intellectual property rights?

It's clearly not a level playing field. However, the U.S. also
takes trade liberties to give its producers an edge in world markets
(See: "A Penchant for Protectionism" later in this chapter). Trade
protectionism isn't the answer. Equitable trade agreements are
reached from a position of strength. Overextended empires spending themselves into bankruptcy with poor economic policies are
not in a position to negotiate favorable "fair trade" treaties.

The global opportunity is knocking, and we have ourselves
to thank for it. The model of capitalism that has helped America thrive is being emulated around the world, but while we've
played a key role in spreading the benefits of the free market,
we can't rest on our laurels. Foreign countries are taking our

lessons to heart, and they're finding ways to compete on our turf. Today's business either answers to the knocking opportunity, or that opportunity will go knocking someplace else. And building walls around a "Fortress America" isn't going to expand our economic pie. Such an approach is a defensive play and ultimately detrimental, as the world will simply trade around us and with each other while our economy stagnates. The following are some trade deals other countries have negotiated among themselves WITHOUT U.S. participation:

> ➢ **European Union/South Korea, 2009**: Covers $96 billion in annual trade.
> ➢ **Canada/Colombia, 2008**: Covers $1.2 billion in annual trade.
> ➢ **Japan/Association of Southeast Asian Nations, 2008**: Covers $211.4 billion in annual trade.[11]

Emerging Economies = Emerging Markets

No one knows specifically where to find the next great marketing bonanza, but you should be able to find emerging marketing opportunities in countries that have a large number of young people who are living their most productive years. Unlike developed countries like the United States, Japan, and the United Kingdom, which have aging populations, upstarts with more youthful populations like Brazil and Ireland are poised to make for dramatic economic gains in the coming decades.

How to Make a Recession Worse

Plants close, jobless claims rise, and unemployed workers face foreclosure on their homes. Too often, politicians make the mistake of thinking that shutting out low-priced imports can protect jobs. After all, reducing the market share of foreign goods should allow more goods from American factories

to be sold, or so the rationale goes. Unfortunately, protectionist trade policies have just the opposite effect. They contribute
to a downward economic spiral for three reasons.

First, other countries may retaliate by refusing import of
American goods into their countries. Such trade sanctions wind
up costing more than they were expected to save by the initial
act of protectionism.

Secondly, the low-priced foreign goods held a place in the
market for a reason; namely, they filled a market need. By taking
away the lower-priced option, families and businesses are denied
the opportunity to lower their costs and obtain the products best
suited for their needs. In short, cost cutting is thwarted, placing
Americans at a further competitive disadvantage globally.

Finally, protectionism enables companies, politicians, and
the public to avoid making difficult decisions regarding necessary changes to recover from economic malaise.

Global Trade Alert, a service of the Centre for Economic
Policy Research (CEPR), reported that protectionist measures
around the world have escalated since the global economic
problems of 2008 surfaced. While considered less widespread
and onerous than the trade protectionist wave of the 1930s,
concern that economic recovery could be hampered if the trend
continued was expressed in the report.[12]

Indeed, to determine whether a recession is facing the prospect of recovery or depression, monitoring the pace and sever-
ity of trade protectionist acts is a key consideration. Fortunately, such information is readily available through organizations
such as the CEPR. The news is not good on this front at this
time, as a "beggar-thy-neighbor" mentality seems to be sweep-
ing the globe. Desperation is driving much of this behavior.
Only time will tell how far this trend will go and the economic
damage it will render.

A Penchant for Protectionism

The following are just some of the protectionist trade measures enacted, along with their subsequent repercussions over an eight-month period:

October 2009: Canada seeks dispute resolution panel from World Trade Organization (WTO) as America's northern neighbor challenges American mandatory country-of-origin labeling law, which it claims unfairly raises the cost of the cattle and hogs its farmers sell into the U.S. market.[13]

September 2009: U.S. places a heavy 35 percent tariff over three years on cheap Chinese tires, cutting the source of nearly 17 percent of tires sold in America. China retaliates by placing trade sanctions against the U.S. for allegedly "dumping" low-priced chickens and auto parts into its country.[14]

September 2009: French president Nicolas Sarkozy proposes a carbon tax on imports from the U.S. and other countries without the carbon policies comparable to those in Europe, following approval by the U.S. House of Representatives of a cap and trade bill levying a carbon tariff on imports.[15]

June 2009: Trade protectionism can take the form of cross-border subsidy wars. Canada's federal parliament grants a nearly $1 billion subsidy to paper mills located within the country. The subsidy is in response to a loophole U.S. paper mills found in highway legislation that allows them (the U.S. paper mills) to obtain some $6 billion in tax credits by burning a byproduct of papermaking. These tax credits allowed U.S. paper mills to lower production costs upwards of 60 percent, threatening the very existence of their Canadian counterparts.[16]

March 2009: The U.S. bans Mexican long-haul truckers from America's highways, in violation of the North American Free Trade Agreement (NAFTA). Mexico retaliates by imposing tariffs ranging from 10 to 45 percent on eighty-nine U.S. products, ranging from California produce to precious metals jewelry.[17]

PREDICTIONS	
Event	*Probability*
More billionaires will reside outside the U.S. than inside it.	95%
The trend away from the U.S. dollar as the world's reserve currency will continue in fits and starts.	90%

The Knock Heard 'Round the World: Winning Strategies for Us, as a Nation

Without a doubt, the worst thing we could do at this crucial point is to erect substantial trade barriers. This would be the equivalent of "kiting" checks (issuing a check and hoping to deposit the money before the check clears) and a classic case of immediate gratification with severe long-term consequences. In this global economy—one which we helped foster—we simply can't afford to shut out the rest of the world.

The only way American workers can support an aging population, while being paid more than foreign workers, is by out-producing, out-competing, and out-thinking their global competitors. We have to improve our population's overall skill set and adapt a global perspective on geography, history, and world economics.

Complaining about unfair competition isn't going to improve or maintain the living standards of most Americans. Well-conceived policies focused on enabling America to win in the global economy are required.

The Knock Heard 'Round the World: Winning Strategies for You, as a Leader

Business leaders can't just think outside the box; you have to think outside the *borders*. It's time to start globe-trotting, looking for BOTH business on foreign soil AND new business ideas in foreign nations that you can bring back and market in the U.S. America does not have a monopoly on ingenuity and entrepreneurial spirit in the world.

> **Gaining a Global Perspective**
> Check out the following sources for a world view on the U.S. economy:
> - *The Financial Times*
> - *The Economist*
> - National Bureau of Economic Research
> - The Sovereign Wealth Fund Institute
> - Global Trade Alert
> - The BBC

With breathtaking new communication, you can now access niche markets anywhere in the world, and you can run a business from the comfort of your own home, in your pajamas, while sipping on your morning coffee. Take networking to an international level!

One underdeveloped business angle is to not only find new markets abroad, but also to service countries that want to do business in the United States. With vast amounts of new imports heading to our shores, you may find companies in need of a liaison on American soil. With the dollar weaker, your services are automatically priced at a discount in other nations.

The Knock 'Round the World: Winning Strategies for You, Personally

Learn a foreign language. Travel, and experience different cultures. After you've made those trips abroad, you'll have a better understanding of global interdependence. You'll literally see why the coming of the Global Innovation Age will not be turned back.

Globalized market opportunities are everywhere and nowhere at the same time. In today's unprecedented global environment, we are literally inventing the blueprint for how this international marketplace will work. In many respects, all of us will be starting from scratch and inventing new ways of gaining the winning edge. The creative, well-skilled individuals, organizations, and nations will thrive. And as for the rest, it appears opportunity will be knocking elsewhere.

Trend 10

Talent Matters —
Do You Have What It Will Take?

The Rising Value of Intellectual Capital

Just as the agricultural society of the late 1800s gave way to the Industrial Age of the 1900s, we're now moving into a post-Industrial Age. In this new age, winners will be determined by their innovation, adaptability, and performance. And what is the essential resource needed for these attributes? The answer is talent.

The need for more talent has been created by a number of macro events. First, technological advancements over the past two decades have increased the demand for highly skilled, tech-savvy workers. Second, the Baby Boomers have begun to retire, and as they leave the workforce, they take with them a stockpile of expertise and experience. Finally, the growing number of highly educated and skilled workers abroad has awakened American organizations to the fact that the best and brightest talent is no longer confined to within the borders of the United States, Western Europe, and Japan.

The quest for talent and its lucrative payoff has created a frenzy that parallels the Gold Rush of 1849. In an issue of *The Economist*, an international survey of top human resource executives indicated that "attracting and retaining talent" had become a top priority, and the majority of companies reported experiencing shortages of talent. *The Economist* also reported that more than 2,300 firms have adopted some sort of talent management technology: Goldman Sachs has a "university"; McKinsey & Company has a "people committee"; and Singapore's Ministry of Manpower has an "international talent division."[1]

To find the true importance of talent, look no further than the bottom line. People with intellectual capital who can impact the profits of a business will dominate the workforce in the years to come. In fact, they've already taken control. Accenture asserts that intangible assets constitute 70 percent of the S&P 500.[2] Those "intangible assets" include intellectual property rights and proprietary processes. It's no longer enough to have a big building; it's the people inside the big building that make the difference.

People with talent will welcome the recruiting efforts of employers, especially after the economy moves beyond the current recession. A meritocracy is already forming, whereby extremely bright individuals with the ability to mobilize a workforce are reaping the top rewards. The success of companies like Google and Apple—in which brilliant minds working as part of teams create highly sought-after innovations—encourage top-level compensation, even during recessionary periods.

In the Global Innovation Age, the emphasis in the U.S. will shift from manufacturing to distribution, design, development, and logistics. To compete in these areas, an employer's most valuable resource will be *intellectual capital*. Talent will matter more than ever, and here is how the world will respond:

The Workforce Requires a Higher Level of Skills

Workers have to be more skilled, adaptable, and independent than ever before. Not only will they need to understand how to use digital tools, but they must also have the ability to manage their own time and productivity. Micro management is a luxury of bygone days.

Independent and adaptable workers who develop their own skill sets will be the workforce of the future. Unskilled workers, who have traditionally relied upon unions to take them under their wing and help them attain a middle-class lifestyle, face serious impediments. There is a glut of low-skilled, hourly workers, and companies simply don't have the time or the payrolls to train a workforce. They want the top level of talent, and they want it now.

Fewer Workers Are Expected to Produce More Work

High-octane performance is a by-product of the Global Innovation Age, and it will be a limiting force to the size of the new economy's labor force. To take performance to even higher levels, fewer people will be expected to accomplish more tasks. Companies no longer have the luxury of hiring specialists for specific roles. Their multidisciplinary workforce will be expected to take multitasking to an entirely new level.

Real-Life Example: Performing to Survive

I once compared the output of my American office with that of a satellite office abroad. The results were jarring. Because of the higher U.S. dollar compared to foreign currencies at the time, my U.S. workers had to produce twice as much as their foreign counterparts to compete. I simply couldn't afford to hire support services or add resources to my American team. Either the U.S. team became more productive and performed more functions, or the company's U.S. operation would lose its competitiveness.

Higher Skills Don't Necessarily Mean Ever-Higher Salaries

Talented people who possess a high level of intellectual capital will be well compensated, but their pay won't be just in the form of a salary. Compensation will be based on performance and contributions to the bottom line. Expect a greater emphasis on profit sharing, bonuses, and employee stock ownership programs.

The meritocracy alluded to earlier in this chapter already embraces this form of compensation. For example, according to an article in the *Wall Street Journal*, Randy Mott, the CIO of Hewlett-Packard, was making a high six-figure salary but could potentially make another five million dollars under a long-term performance bonus plan.[3]

Low-Tech Manufacturing Jobs Lost in the Last Decade Are Gone for Good

America only needs to look at its own history to understand this sobering trend. In 1900, nearly one-third of Americans made their living from farming. Today, that number is under 1 percent and still shrinking.[4] Manufacturing workers will encounter a similar fate. In fact, they already are.

Look at the decline of traditional mass-production manufacturing jobs to see the proof. Workers in America's manufacturing sector are crying foul, claiming that jobs are being lost overseas to countries that pay lower wages and have subpar working conditions.

They're right, but they're also missing the big picture. Workers must understand that manufacturing jobs *overall* are vanishing as worldwide manufacturing productivity grows. Between 1995 and 2002, manufacturing employment worldwide

"... creativity trumps other leadership characteristics. Creative leaders are comfortable with ambiguity and experimentation. To connect with and inspire a new generation, they (creative leaders) lead and interact in entirely new ways."—2010 IBM Global CEO Study

declined an estimated twenty to thirty million jobs, roughly 11–16 percent, while overall production rose. China—well known for the growth of its manufacturing sector—lost approximately seventeen million factory jobs during this period, while productivity surged 60 percent.[5]

Traditional Positions Are Being Redefined

Businesses are now revisiting traditional job functions and making them more cross functional. Creativity, as it applies to performance, innovation, and adaptability, is becoming more recognized as an invaluable talent. Due to the high level of complexity uncertainty and change inherent with global innovation, creative leadership is essential to find new ways to succeed rather than following well-established approaches.

The migration of roles from traditional methodologies to multi-tasking, intuitive approaches will lead to the elimination of the types of jobs used to support those traditional functions. Routine, repetitive jobs that can be replaced by a computer chip or a low-paid offshore worker are in real danger.

The trend is clear: The labor force will be geared to those who possess the highest degree of skill and talent. It's a paradigm shift that will not be limited to individuals. It will also impact institutions—from businesses to entire nations.

New Roles for Top Management

Talent will affect every job in an organization, starting at the top. Old, well-defined roles in organizations are being redefined into fluid, ever-evolving new positions. Here are some examples:

> ➤ **Human Resource Officers** tended to focus on programs and policies. Now they're becoming Chief Talent Strategists. Their top priorities are to align talent with

corporate strategies and determining how these talent pools will work throughout an organization.

> **Chief Information Officers** once maintained computer systems. Now, as Chief Technology Officers, they must determine ways to use technology to a company's strategic advantage. For example, a company website used to be nothing more than a digital brochure. Now a CTO will be charged with transitioning it into a profit center.

> **Chief Financial Officers** will move from accounting roles to Chief Asset Managers and will determine how company assets can be deployed to build revenue and cut costs.

As these and other top management positions change, other functions will be transformed throughout the organization. If a position can't be shown to contribute to the bottom line, it becomes a likely candidate for elimination or outsourcing.

Winners and Losers

Let's take a brief look at which workers, leaders, businesses, and nations will thrive and which will be lucky to survive during the Global Innovation Age.

Workers and leaders who will thrive:
The future favors workers and leaders who are creative thinkers and possess multiple skills. These people are always thinking of ways to improve processes and bring more value to a business. They are willing to be paid based on their performance, and constantly looking to improve their skills and embrace technological advancement.

Workers and leaders lucky to survive:
The workers that cling to their job descriptions and leaders with a "silo" mentality focused only on their specific functional area will be lucky to make it through the Global Innovation Age. These people tend to perform the same basic tasks day in and day out. They are resistant to change and rarely look to expand their skills. They spend most of their time worrying about losing their jobs instead of thinking of ways to add value to the bottom line.

(Continued)

Businesses that will thrive:
For successful businesses of the future, technology and a focus on workforce adaptability will continue to eliminate clerical and administrative functions. Workers will be more cross functional and collaborative, and processes will be more customer-focused. Traditional roles will thus be redefined, from top-level executives to frontline workers. Employees will be engaged in ways to impact the bottom line and paid based on their performance.

Businesses lucky to survive:
Dying businesses will cling to the notion that they have the right product but just need to find a customer who will buy it. These companies will move slowly, guided by an organizational hierarchy layered in bureaucracy and resistant to change. These organizations will continue to revolve around job descriptions, not talent pools. Plant managers will police employees, Human Resources will focus on programs and policies, and employees will be stuck with their set salaries and prescribed job functions.

Nations who will thrive:
Successful nations will actively participate in the global economy. They will place priority on developing intellectual capital, primarily through education and minimizing uncertainty and complexity in terms of government programs and policies. If homegrown talent does not exist, these nations will loosen their immigration policies to draw in the best and the brightest. They will produce thriving, well-to-do populaces who value higher education and upward mobility.

Nations lucky to survive:
The nations that will decline during the Global Innovation Age will adopt a protectionist stance. They will resist the pull of the global economy, restricting immigration of foreigners, including those with intellectual capital. Strong labor unions and government bureaucracies will ardently defend the status quo. Education will be marginalized, and the chasm will grow further between the wealthy population and poorly educated workers with low skill levels.

PREDICTIONS	
Event	*Probability*
A larger percentage of employee compensation will be directly linked to financial performance of the employer or productivity of employees. This will be a growing trend.	90%
Those workers with the highest levels of education and skills will generally maintain or improve their standard of living (barring hyperinflation or an economic depression), while unskilled workers will increasingly turn to unions and political activism to offset the economic pressures they face.	80%

Talent Matters: Winning Strategies for Us, as a Nation

America needs all the brainpower it can lay its hands on. In the age of post-Industrial global competition, as fiercely fought as any war, the nations with the most intellectual capital have the edge as new ideas keep streaming forth to replace those fallen into obsolescence.

Hostility toward educated, talented, and entrepreneurial immigrants is self-defeating, as those immigrants turned away from our shores will put their talents to work for the "other side." Building walls around America will only isolate us. Instead, it would behoove us to encourage the smartest and most talented people to come to "our side."

Talent Matters: Winning Strategies for You, as a Leader

Your top priority in the Global Innovation Age will be to constantly develop talent. You can't wait until you have an opening to fill. Instead of thinking in terms of job roles, think about talent pools. Recruit people who can thrive in the Global Innovation Age—people who exhibit the characteristics we've highlighted throughout this chapter.

Real-Life Example:
Education and Global Competitive Advantage

A friend of mine, who just returned from a trip through southeast Asia, recited being told by his host in Singapore how the host's children in preschool were bringing home six hours of homework every day. Just throwing more money at our public schools or trying to legislate educational outcomes will not add more value to America's reserves of intellectual capital. Radical change requires a focus on developing students' individual strengths and interests and then implementing a world-class education that allows graduates to out-think, out-create, and out-perform their foreign competitors.

Managing this talent pool on an organizational basis is critical. Your workers' skills should complement each other. For example, a creative thinker might need to be paired with a detail-oriented taskmaster. Don't staff your talent pools based solely on your needs for today. Instead, consider your company's long-term objectives. What kind of talent will you need to take you there?

Developing the talent you need may be necessary versus hiring needed talent. Due to the demand for highly specialized skills and the shortage of such specialists, finding the perfectly qualified candidate may be exceptionally difficult. An alternative route is to select job candidates who are "teachable fits." That is, people with related skills who can be trained to acquire the highly specialized skills needed.

Finally, reconsider how your organization is structured. Does talent really matter in your company? Do your people think in terms of adding value to the bottom line, or do they focus on preserving their turf? To make the transition, people must be

> **Current Recession Masks Imminent Talent Gap**
>
> ". . . 40 percent of workers now entering the workforce have not earned any college credits. Furthermore, record numbers of workers with college degrees are not choosing so-called STEM careers in science, technology, engineering, and mathematics."—Edward Gordon[6]

> **Talent Mismatch**
>
> "As we emerge from the recession, we will face another challenge: finding the right talent. Despite the global recession and the weakest employment outlook in decades, employers are nonetheless facing a shortage of talent in critical areas."[7]

rewarded for their adaptability, performance, and innovation.

To really differentiate your organization and aim for the quantum leap past your competition, encourage risk-taking by your workforce. Reward success, of course, but also make an attempt to view failure as constructive under the right circumstances (the right circumstances would include a timely and well executed initiative that included a well-defined contingency plan). Innovation requires risk-taking. Risk-taking requires training, empowerment, and boldness. Playing it safe with incremental improvements won't allow your organization to take the lead in the Global Innovation Age. Creative leadership will encourage an organizational culture that supports calculated risk-taking.

Talent Matters: Winning Strategies for You, Personally

The Global Innovation Age will require courage from all of us and include its fair share of anxiety. Job insecurity, global competition, and learning new skills aren't as cozy as a stable job with a predictable paycheck.

Everyone, regardless of their position in the company, must develop their own talent. Your own education should never stop. You must constantly enhance your skills by acquiring an advanced degree, a trade, a foreign language, or some other valued skill set. In the Global Innovation Age, technology trends are crucial. Build on your ability to understand and manipulate tools of the digital world.

If you're a manager, your job is changing too. Focus less on people management and more on performance management.

Remember, a new, highly independent workforce is emerging. Find ways to let them flourish and work cohesively together—even if they're not in the same office space. The labor market will favor those who can generate new revenue streams and allocate resources to take advantage of market changes.

> Future success will not be based on the size of your plant or the equipment inside your building; it will be dictated by your company's ability to mobilize intellectual capital.

Be sure to possess basic financial skills. Accounting is the language of business, and an understanding of financial statements is crucial. This skill doesn't apply just to business. Non-profits require the same understanding, and hard-pressed voters are already demanding elected officials do a better job of managing public finances. If you understand even basic finance, then you can understand how you can help drive performance. That's intellectual capital in action. Ask yourself two questions:

- ➢ Why does my job, department, or business exist (that is, what are people paying me to do)?
- ➢ How do I contribute to the bottom line and objectives of the organization?

Answer each of the above questions in just one or two sentences. If you are unable to do so, start re-thinking what you are doing. Otherwise, you are at risk of becoming collateral damage in the war for control of the future.

PART THREE:
HOW TO WIN IN THE
NEW ECONOMY

<u>Your</u> Plan B

Winning Strategies

Remember, *the world is changing, not coming to an end.* The challenge lies in dealing with America's transformation to a post-Industrial Age world, encompassing the complexity, uncertainty, and constant change that global innovation presents. Your options and their consequences include the following:

➤ Prepare yourself and your organization. Monitor key trends, think proactively, become more resourceful, and develop contingency plans to maintain an updated Plan B. This approach will lead to successful strategies.

Or, you can . . .

➤ Play it safe and follow along with the status quo and Industrial Age premises. This is a great way to get left behind.

Or, you can . . .

➤ Do nothing and just hope things will return to "normal." Pursuing this option could wipe out your career, your retirement funding, and your organization.

This book has portrayed ten major challenges facing you and your organization as America transitions to the Global Innovation Age. You may have found some content of this book a bit unsettling. The goal has not been to depress or discourage you, but to help you prepare a winning plan of action. A world of opportunity awaits the creative and aggressive.

Past Assumptions of Economic and Political Order No Longer Apply

The U.S. is still an economic powerhouse, but with few exceptions, what worked in the past won't work in the future. For sure, the approaches that failed in the past will fail again in the future. The empty promises and assurances of those with a vested interest in maintaining the status quo cannot change such realities.

Be prepared to do tasks you have never had to do before and anticipate that events will take place that will scuttle past assumptions. For instance, owning gold stocks may seem like a winner, but the government can change that. During the Great Depression, President Roosevelt passed laws making gold ownership illegal for private citizens. Could it happen again?

> **The American Opera**
> American history is an operatic story of looming disaster averted in unanticipated, improbable events orchestrated by daring leaders.

Well, the IRS has issued notice that silver and gold bullion are considered "collectibles," not investments, and any long-term gain from such a sale shall be taxed as ordinary income, not the lower capital gains rate. This rule applies to shares in exchange-traded funds (ETFs) that hold gold and silver bullion as well. The message is clear: The rules can and will be changed to benefit those with the power to do so for their own benefit.

Win by Following the Trends

The ten trends discussed in this book should be among your top priorities to address in creating a Plan B.

The Contingency Plan *IS* the Plan: Global inter-connections increase complexity, uncertainty, and change. Are you prepared to deal with the new realities?

"Brother, Can You Spare a Trillion Dollars?": Money is a global commodity, but it is in short supply as the world wrestles with the de-leveraging of financial excesses. Think like a global money manager and "follow the money." Are you limiting yourself to U.S. sources for investors, buyers, and lenders?

Healthcare on Life Support: Put aside ideology and dependency on any third party when it comes to your medical care. Are you aggressively managing the health of you and your family like a precious, world-class asset?

China Stands Up: The Red Giant has colossal challenges as well as growth potential. What's your strategy for positioning yourself to compete, and collaborate, effectively?

The Employed, the Under-Employed, and the Unemployable: By perpetuating Industrial Age expectations, America has fostered a growing underclass and unaffordable compensation plans for union and government workers. Millions of Americans are unemployed while employers find key jobs hard to fill. It's getting tougher for you to grow. How will you respond?

America's Spending Binge: To keep the economic game rolling, both political parties have encouraged the private sector to join government leaders in "living large." Now the credit card is just about maxed out and the statements are being sent out to you for payment. What are you going to do?

Prices Gone Wild: Prices are caught in the cross currents of global inflationary and deflationary forces. We are entering an era that will play havoc with spot prices. How will you plan, save, and invest in an era when prices are unpredictable?

The Demographic Time Bomb: You hear it ticking. With each passing day, more Baby Boomers are hitting retirement age. The funding to preserve Social Security and Medicare for them will fall short. How will you and your organization cope with the ramifications of this demographic shift?

The Knock Heard 'Round the World: Global markets outside the U.S. are growing and offer extraordinary opportunities. Trade protectionism can turn some of those opportunities away. What steps do you need to take to capitalize on globalism?

Talent Matters: Contrary to conventional wisdom, knowledge itself is not power. Power comes from the ability to APPLY knowledge. Talent is the ability to apply knowledge and skill creatively and effectively. What's your strategy for developing the talent you need?

Win by Anticipating the "Tipping Point"

As a general statement, watch for how trends grow in ways that defy conventional wisdom—either in small increments and/or in large parabolic moves—to a tipping point, similar to that described by Malcolm Gladwell,[1] causing a snowball effect whereby a large reaction occurs. For instance, taxes may be in a rising trend and absorbed in the economy. However, if taxes suddenly make a substantially bigger jump than in the past, the level of taxation may likely have snowballed to the point where taxpayers revolt and/or related government revenue decreases.

Key Areas to Monitor

The Economy

- ➤ **Tax rates**: Refer to your property tax bill, sales tax rate, and income tax rate, as well as charges for government services such as garbage pickup.
- ➤ **Interest rates:** Mortgage rates and CD rates can be followed on Bankrate.com and in the *Wall Street Journal*. Treasury bond rates can be tracked on many financial websites, such as www.MarketWatch.com.
- ➤ **Trade protectionism:** Trade measures taken by countries can be followed on Global Trade Alert reports issued by the Centre for Economic Policy Research (CEPR) at www.GlobalTradeAlert.org
- ➤ **The value of the U.S. dollar:** Track the value of the dollar via the Internet using these two ETFs: Powershares DB US Dollar (symbol UUP) and SPDR Gold Trust (Symbol GLD).

Government and Society

- ➤ **Government policies and their impact:** Keep it simple and subscribe to *The Kiplinger Letter* at KiplingerBiz.com.

War

- ➤ **Afghanistan, Iraq, and the War on Terror:** Political correctness will not win these wars. Is the political class in Washington supporting victory on the battlefront, or getting in the way?
- ➤ **More and bigger wars:** Iran's mullahs might start a war to distract their disgruntled populace. And let us not forget the matter of North Korea's desire to become a manufacturer and distributor of nukes to anyone who hates America. Have you noticed that Bolivia has gone Marxist, along with Venezuela and Cuba?

The World

> **What's Happening in China, India, and other major developing countries:** Reference *The Economist* (www.economist.com) and *The Wall Street Journal* (www.WSJ.com).

A Checklist of Events to Monitor

If you do nothing else, be on the lookout for these events:

☐ Interest rates start rising, and taxes are significantly increased. (Obviously, this is not a good thing.)

☐ Trade protectionism continues and worsens. (Monitor this closely; a trade war would be devastating to the U.S. economy.)

☐ Nations devalue their currency in relation to others in order to make their exports more affordable in other countries. (This "race to the bottom" signals desperation of central bankers around the world.)

☐ Credit for small business and individuals tightens. (Remember, it takes credit to acquire and grow.)

☐ Government keeps passing new laws and regulations that dramatically raise costs to businesses and individuals. (This is especially bad if it occurs in conjunction with more government control of business.)

☐ Laws and regulations are put into place that loosen voter registration requirements and limit government critics. (This will lead to political instability and abuses.)

☐ An increase in the use of quid pro quo deals, whereby organizations receive government funding or other benefits in exchange for political support. (A major risk of increased corruption.)

☐ Government officials exempt themselves from programs and regulations that apply to the general public. In other words, a "Do as I say, not as I do" attitude keeps growing among elected officials. (When the double standard grows to extremes, it shows arrogance and contempt by the leaders for the people.)

☐ The U.S. dollar is dropped as the world's reserve currency and/ or foreign countries announce they will no longer buy U.S. debt.

☐ Another unimaginable event happens, such as a major terrorist attack like 9/11, or America withdraws its troops from Afghanistan. (In effect, this will represent losing the war.)

(Continued)

☐ You notice inflation or deflation becoming significant in your own life.
☐ China's economy begins to falter.

Develop Winning Strategies

This book does not recommend you go out and load up on gold coins, create an arsenal, or hunker down in some out-of-the-way cave. Nor should you cash out of everything or bet everything on a particular type of asset or investment. Rather, you are urged to *re-think* how you invest, borrow, save, and spend.

America is caught between the forces of deflation and inflation, political power plays, and globalism. We may just muddle along experiencing episodic panic attacks. On the other hand, if the politicians panic, a series of economic crises could erupt as governments desperately seek a "silver bullet" to implement with the primary goal to stay in power.

The objective is to strategically position yourself and your organization in order to survive and succeed, no matter what the scenario. Your Plan B should include a strategy to go on the offense to gain advantage from the changes and upheaval taking place, and a defensive strategy for when events turn against you and an orderly strategic retreat is necessary to regroup and try again another day.

What You Don't Need to Do . . . and Should Do

Do you need to move to a locale far away from a city to avoid being in the target area of terrorist threats, nuclear attack, or marauding gangs of thugs? NO.

Do you need to flee the country? NO (unless you're a felon or child molester).

Many people still recall the public concern of an atomic bomb attack in the 1960s, and specifically how that concern led many people to build bomb shelters. The bomb shelters were never needed for the dreaded worst-case scenario. They wound up becoming fruit cellars, marijuana hideaways, and death traps for children.

A few words are in order regarding the option of leaving the U.S. and living in another country. Despite the risks and uncertainty facing us at home, relocating outside the U.S. is simply not a viable option for many people. Such a move should be a thoroughly researched decision based on making your life better and more enjoyable. After all, there are downsides to living outside the U.S. that may not be apparent when you take a relaxing vacation to your personal paradise.

Renouncing U.S. citizenship is another action to avoid. Changing citizenship is something only the super-rich with the bulk of their income and assets outside the U.S. should consider. Even then, more than taxes have to be taken into account—namely, the time you'll be allowed to reside stateside will be limited to avoid U.S. taxation. This can become an issue if you need extensive specialized healthcare (from American doctors), have a tremendous opportunity requiring your presence, or wish to spend a few months with a dying parent.

Another good reason for not packing up and shipping out: You can't run away from your problems. . . and you may just be trading one set of problems for another. America's problems are your problems because it's your government, but ultimately it's up to you whether to flee or fight.

What you do need is a home in a place that provides a comfortable middle ground that will allow you to survive a worst-case scenario but not be left behind if the situation turns around for the better. As stated at the beginning of this chapter, this book is not preaching Armageddon. Rather, the objective is to make you aware of the potential dangers, what to anticipate as events and trends develop, and to position yourself with the flexibility, knowledge, and means to take advantage of whatever scenario appears.

A Checklist for Your Safety and Security

Every home, office, and business should be outfitted to survive storms, power outages, and natural catastrophes, as well as any potential global meltdown of one sort or another. We're talking about being prepared for all types of emergencies. Yet, many families and organizations are totally unprepared for such events. Where life becomes increasingly unstable, emergency preparedness becomes increasingly vital. Just do it! Here are some items you should have on hand:

- ☐ Diesel fuel, natural gas, or propane-powered generator for home
- ☐ First aid kit with extra dressings and iodine or other antiseptics
- ☐ A month's supply (or more) of required prescription medicines
- ☐ Multiple vitamins, aspirin, and other assorted pain relievers
- ☐ Bottled water
- ☐ Extra batteries
- ☐ Radio and portable TV
- ☐ A week's worth of canned and dried food
- ☐ Basic utensils, including can and bottle openers, pots and pans
- ☐ Spare blankets
- ☐ Rolls of coins
- ☐ Sewing kit and safety pins
- ☐ Duct tape, toilet paper, paper towels, rope, and matches
- ☐ Multi-purpose pocket knife
- ☐ Basic tools including pliers, hammer, screwdriver, etc.
- ☐ Hand sanitizer
- ☐ Pocket notebook with spare pens
- ☐ Candles, especially those for cooking, flashlight
- ☐ Firewood (even if you don't have a fireplace)

Your Plan B:
Winning Strategies for Your Community, State, and Country

The purpose of this book is not to pontificate on how the author would "fix" the country's problems. Rather, the intent is to provide an understanding of our dilemma in transitioning to the Age of Global Innovation and what can be done to survive and succeed. The required leadership isn't likely to come from the ranks of the established political elite, but from people like you. (A useful rule of thumb is to never underestimate the American people and never overestimate the politicians.) While you may not be running a state or country, your willingness and ability to apply your Plan B effectively to anticipate the future, develop the necessary resources, and be prepared with a contingency plan can be valuable in the following ways:

> ➤ **Demand and support policies** that will make America more competitive and financially sound; enhance our nation's intellectual capital; and prepare Americans for the Global Innovation Age.
>
> ➤ **Vote** for candidates who have the knowledge and backbone to be honest brokers and make tough decisions.
>
> ➤ **Take matters into your own hands** by implementing some of your own solutions to the problems addressed in this book. For instance:
>
> - Contact schools to speak with, or tutor, students on the skill sets they will need in order to succeed in life.
> - Arrange for your business to fund vouchers for parents of children in failed schools to attend school(s) of their choice.
> - Organize or participate in groups and businesses to provide relief services in the event of catastrophic events.
> - Get in the network. In a politicized economy (which we most certainly have), being networked with the political establishment will be helpful, even if it is only in the role of an "interested constituent."

<u>Your</u> Plan B:
Winning Strategies for You, as a Leader

Winning organizations will be those able to develop teams and networks of talented and skilled people who can drive strat-

egy, not just fulfill job descriptions. Success will be less a result of incremental
improvement and more dependent on
opportunistic leaps beyond where the
market or competition stands.

> In the Global Innovation Age, think in terms of going "beyond-the-art," not just state-of-the-art, to achieve a quantum leap in competitive advantage.

Become More Resourceful

> ➤ Assess the intellectual capital at your organization and compare it to what the organization needs in order to succeed.
> ➤ Monitor trends—it's essential.
> ➤ Ask your employees what they think of the economy. They can provide a surprisingly valuable assessment. Anecdotal information can prove as useful as hard data.
> ➤ Review your core business lines and strategies for unexpected turns in business. Determine multiple revenue plateaus and attach a survival strategy to each one.
> ➤ Go beyond your current competitors and look at potential competition from outside your industry.
> ➤ Travel internationally and take note of what is happening in the economies of the nations you visit. Watch for potential ideas to bring home and markets you could potentially enter.
> ➤ Determine if your business model is still current and vital.
> ➤ What policies do you have in place to encourage your staff to innovate?

Anticipate, Don't Just React

> ➤ Be proactive, and mean it. It will not be enough to cut costs to match prices, for instance. It will be necessary, for example, to have a Plan B in place for cost reduction by anticipating possible future price cuts.

> ➤ Diversify your markets and sourcing. In the late Industrial Age, a major thrust was toward consolidating suppliers. However, the Great Recession taught the lesson that along with such concentration comes the risk of default and extended lead times in the supply chain. In the Global Innovation Age, war (whether cyber espionage or physical destruction of infrastructure) must be factored in when considering worldwide logistics.

Develop a Contingency Plan for Survival

> ➤ "We couldn't have imagined something like this happening!" just isn't going to cut it anymore. Your company needs a set of survival and emergency response plans for virtually any type of catastrophe that can happen. The global nature of business brings not only new and different opportunities to your door, but problems as well.

Your Plan B:
Winning Strategies for You, Personally

Anticipate trends, strengthen your resources, lead creatively, and create a contingency plan—all of these same steps apply to you and your family as well as your business. Anticipate your income becoming less predictable and take the following actions:

> ➤ Live within your means (Gasp!) and put your personal financial house in order. If you do nothing else, start living within your take-home pay and put aside at least 10 percent of your paycheck into savings.
> ➤ If you stand to lose everything from losing your job or taking a substantial pay cut, you need to change your lifestyle. Having no cash and a mountain of bills with no means to pay them will place you in the category of

"collateral damage" in the economic battles ahead, and that is not a category you want to be in.

Granted, the government MAY try to bail out those in deep financial water, and hyperinflation can make debt based on FIXED rates virtually disappear. However, just ask the homeowners underwater on their adjustable rate mortgages whether it is easy to resolve such problems, even with a government-mandated mortgage "workout" plan with the banks.

Real-Life Example: The Middle-Class Blues

I recently made a delivery to a food pantry. The people standing in line to have a turn at picking up second-hand or unsold grocery items weren't just the poor and/or dispossessed. One of the pantry volunteers explained how two-income, middle-class families have suddenly found themselves with no money left over for food after paying the mortgage, utility bills, and car payments when one of the family members was laid off.

The leveraged life can allow you to live large for a while—until unplanned setbacks show up. Middle-class Americans can't print more money to bail themselves out. The politicians reserve that right for themselves.

Diversify Your Investments

Own more than a house and some stocks. From 2007–10, we saw these two investment categories tumble. In fact, during the financial panic at that time, virtually every asset class dropped as investors sought cash. Focus on spreading investments across the following asset categories as part of a financial contingency plan, and allocate your funds among them based on your anticipation of events from monitoring the trends mentioned earlier in this chapter.

> ➤ **Real estate:** Invest in income-producing real estate, but not necessarily residential rental units, as politicians

have been known to slap rent controls on landlords of residential properties during inflationary periods.

➢ **Cash**: Also consider money market accounts and bank savings accounts. Keep twice as much as you would ordinarily have on hand tucked away at home. Strive to have enough cash available to cover your cost of living for one year.

➢ **Stocks**: Invest in stocks of well-established companies that pay high dividends, so you may earn a good return on your money even if the value of the stock goes down. Historically, average dividend yields of 6 to 7 percent on the S&P 500 Stock Index have marked "once-in-a-lifetime" buying opportunities.

➢ **Gold and precious metals.** Consider placing up to 10 percent of your portfolio in this category, with purchases only when precious metals have experienced a pullback in price. Add a few coins if you can obtain them at a reasonable price, which may be difficult while the global economy is in turmoil. Additional purchases beyond the 10 percent should be predicated on governments around the world moving toward devaluing their currencies and running printing presses on overtime.

➢ **Bonds**: During inflation, bonds tend to drop in value. "Buy-and-hold" doesn't apply to bonds anymore either.

➢ **Foreign stocks and bonds:** This category involves market timing. In a global economy, if the U.S. market collapses, the rest of the world will be sucked into the pit as well. Also, if the U.S. dollar rises in value, foreign holdings will be impacted negatively.

➢ **Foreign real estate**: Invest only in a friendly nation with strong property rights and some fiscal discipline such as Canada, New Zealand, or Australia. You can purchase ETFs with international real estate interests.

> **A small business:** A business that is online and has international markets is ideal. Consider cash businesses, or where revenue is paid up front.

Gold and Silver Tips

In the unlikely event the economy collapses and you need to use your physical gold to buy the necessities of life, a one-ounce gold coin could be worth thousands of dollars at that point. Unfortunately, it can be problematic if you're trying to get change for that after buying a Big Mac Value Meal.

This is where gold jewelry comes into the picture. A link from a gold necklace that's only part of an ounce can be more easily exchanged for goods or even cash.

Following is a rough rule of thumb for converting carats into gold, assuming the jewelry is solid gold and not plated or partially filled with another material:

> Fourteen-carat is 56 percent gold

> Eighteen-carat is 75 percent gold

> Twenty-four-carat is 100 percent gold

Another option for smaller transactions is to acquire silver coins or low denomination gold coins, which can be purchased in as small as one-twentieth of an ounce. Finally, rolls of U.S. quarters and nickels minted before 1965 contain .071 ounces of silver per dollar of face value and are available through coin dealers.

Acquire More Resources to Draw Upon

➤ Make sure you possess a strong set of marketable skills.

➤ Volunteer to work in non-profit organizations and to network as broadly as possible.

➤ Track those with a major advantage in terms of global innovation and team up with them when possible.

➤ Develop a team of advisors and mentors.

➤ Upgrade and expand your skills via education, especially certifications.

Winning the War for Control of Your Future

We have many of challenges ahead of us. America's transition from the Industrial Age to a Global Innovation Age is far from complete. This transition will be tumultuous as Industrial Age institutions push back to retain their positions while wealth and power are dispersed more widely around the globe.

The trends in this book have identified problems to be addressed, but these problems are also opportunities for those who can provide solutions to them. For those who are flexible and resourceful with well-developed skills and talent, globalism is exponentially increasing potential markets. Timing will be important. The willingness and ability to take on more risk and push harder to win will be essential.

America has faced difficult, dispiriting times before, but recovery is possible. In July 1979, President Jimmy Carter gave what came to be known as his "Malaise Speech." At the time, America was suffering. Oil imports were controlled by a cartel of foreign countries determined to boost their profits regardless of the impact on Americans. Gas and heating fuels were in short supply. Long lines would form at gas stations, and the drivers hoped the supply didn't run out before it was their turn at the pump. Inflation was in the double digits, and the economy was in a recession. News reports commonly referred to the "Misery Index," a measurement of the combined effect of high inflation and unemployment. Americans were being held hostage in Iran, but America's military seemed powerless to rescue them.

> **Normal's Gone**
> It would have been easier to write a book advising readers to tighten up, tweak a few things, and tough it out until the return of Normal. But Normal doesn't live here anymore and isn't coming back. Complexity, Uncertainty, and Constant Change have moved in and show no signs of leaving anytime soon.

During his speech, President Carter told the American public how the world had changed and we had no choice but to accept austerity and sacrifice. To deal with the situation, the government would handle matters. More czars would be appointed to manage the economy. Mandates would be handed down. Our role as citizens was to accept the situation, pay more taxes to support the government, and be cheerleaders for our public officials.

Jimmy Carter's presidency never recovered, and Carter lost his bid for re-election in a humiliating defeat in 1980. Leadership matters. America will require leadership of epic proportions as the country redefines its expectations and role in the world.

Faster economic growth, by itself, will not allow America to grow out of its problems. The problems are structural and institutional. Millions of Americans are unprepared to deal with the demands of the Global Innovation Age. Still more millions of public sector employees, union workers, and university academicians have a false sense of security—they wrongly believe their retirement pensions and benefit programs are assured. Even more millions of Baby Boomers in the private sector are going to find their dreams of an affluent, comfortable retirement placed on hold. An entrenched and inept political class is running out of superficial maneuvers to maintain the pretense that all is well along the battlefront.

Winning the war for control of your future requires an objective approach to the realities of the Global Innovation Age. Major institutions based on Industrial Age thinking will fail. The Guardians of the Status Quo will wring their hands with empathy but cannot be counted on for solutions. Power struggles will be of epic proportions. Identify your winning strategies and prepare your Plan B to turn the complexity, uncertainty, and constant change of the Global Innovation Age to your advantage. Most of all, act decisively when the time comes . . . and win in the new economy.

Appendix

How Much Is a Trillion Dollars?

"A billion here, a billion there, and pretty soon you're talking real money," quipped the late Senator Everett Dirksen.[1] Today, a puny billion dollars is just the tip of the iceberg. Now, trillions of dollars are bandied about when it comes to U.S. government spending. The numbers are so large they are hard to conceive.

To start with, a trillion dollars is 1,000 billion dollars or a million million dollars. It would take a million millionaires (with a hypothetical net worth of exactly one million dollars each) to give up their money to fund one trillion dollars. In the context of the roughly 114 million households[2] and 140 million

---

[1] http://online.wsj.com/article/SB123120542333456031.html. January 6, 2009. However, the Dirksen Center has not been able to confirm the quote in its entirety. DirksenCenter.org/print_billionhere.html (Accessed March 21, 2010)

[2] Day, Jennifer Cheeseman, *Projections of the Number of Households and Families in the United States: 1995 to 2010, U.S.* Bureau of the Census, Current Population Reports, p. 25–1129, U.S. Government Printing Office, Washington D.C., 1996.

individual tax returns filed[3] in America, based on 2010 projections, a trillion dollars amounts to about:
  ➤ $8,696 per household
  ➤ $7,143 for every individual tax return filed
The national debt of the United States by 2010 was over $12
trillion.[4] But that's chump change compared to Social Security
and Medicare. According to the Social Security and Medicare
Trustees 2009 Reports, the total long-range, unfunded liabilities
of these two programs alone amount to $107 trillion, not ad-
justed for inflation.[5] Yes, that's "trillion," not "billion."

Perhaps the following will help you to visualize and under-
stand how much a trillion dollars amounts to. A trillion dollars:
  ➤ Consisting of $100 bills laid end to end would stretch
    966,698 miles
  ➤ Would take 32,000 years to pay off at the rate of $1 per
    second
  ➤ Would be more than one million dollars spent each day
    since the birth of Christ (Actually, a million dollars a day
    for the past 2009 years amounts to "only" about $733
    billion.)
  ➤ Amounts to $3,436 for every man, woman, and child in
    America[6]

[3] Based on "Table 469. Individual Income Tax Returns Filed," U.S. Internal Revenue Service, IRS
Data Book, annual (Publication 55B), www.census.gov/compendia/statab/2010/tables/10s0469.
pdf (Accessed October 4, 2010).
[4] U.S.DebtClock.org, March 21, 2010.
[5] Social Security and Medicare Trustees Report 2009, SSA.gov/OACT/TR 5/12/2009 and
Villarreal, Pam, "Social Security and Medicare Projections: 2009," June 11, 2009, NCPA.org/pub/ba662.
(Accessed March 21, 2010)
[6] U.S. Census Bureau, Census.gov/popest/national/national/html. (Accessed March 21, 2010)

What could you do with a trillion dollars? Well, you could live pretty good for a year on just the interest earned in ONE day on a trillion dollars (amounting to $164,835)[7] and use the rest of the money to address some social issues you are concerned about. For example, a trillion dollars would:

> - Buy five million Americans a $200,000 home (doesn't it make you wonder why there are any homeless people left in the country?)
> - Purchase enough food to last a year for the estimated 842 million people in the world who don't have enough to eat.[8]
> - Fund a $63,000 scholarship for each of the 15.9 million students enrolled in American colleges and universities.[9]

[7] Calculated at 6 percent interest rate based on Composite Corporate Bond Rate issued by Internal Revenue Service. IRS.gov/retirement/article/0,,id=123229,00. html (Accessed March 21, 2010)
[8] Calculated by dividing $1 trillion by 842 million. The resulting $1,200 per person, on average, should purchase sufficient food to eliminate hunger around the world for a year. This calculation does not take into account food distribution issues. Estimate of hungry people is based on the World Bank Report 2009
[9] U.S. Census Bureau, Census.gov/Press-Release/www/releases/archives/facts_for_features_special July 26, 2004. (Accessed March 21, 2010)

References and Notes

Trend 1: The Contingency Plan *IS* the Plan

1. "World's Cheapest Car Goes on Show," *BBC News*, January 10, 2008. http://news.bbc.co.uk/2/hi/business/7180396.stm.

2. Aeppel, Timothy, "Show Stopper: How Plastic Popped the Cork Monopoly," *The Wall Street Journal*, May 1, 2010, p.A1.

3. Berman, Saul F., Christner, Richard, and Bell, Ragna, "After the Crisis, What Now?" [Executive Report] IBM Global Business Services, March 2010. Analysis provided by authors incorporating the work of Nissam Nicholas Taleb from *The Black Swan: The Impact of the Highly Improbable* and further analysis by L.A. Jenkins (for this book).

4. Harvard Management Update, "How to Think Strategically in a Recession," *Harvard Business Review*, "Best Practices Blog," February 26, 2008. http://discussionleader.hbsp.com/hmu/2008/02/how-to-think-strategically-in.php (Accessed October 3, 2010).

5. Hardy, Quentin, "Radio Google," Forbes.com, November 26, 2007. http://members.forbes.com/forbes/2007/1126/048_print.html (Accessed August 3, 2010).

6. Holden, Reed and Burton, Mark, "Five Pricing Strategies for Companies During a Recession," *Small Business Digest*, March 2, 2009. http://www.2sbdigest.com/Five-Pricing-Strategies (Accessed September 1, 2010).

7. Lee, Hendry, "Five Recession-Proof Strategies," Enspiro Consulting Group, December 2008. http://www.enspiroconsulting.com/articles_detail.php?case_arti_id=54 (Accessed October 3, 2010).

Trend 2: "Brother, Can You Spare a Trillion Dollars?"
1. "Who Will Pay for America's Bailout?" *MoneyWeek* magazine (UK), September 24, 2009.

2. Cao, Judy and Chen, Judy, "China's Premier Wen 'Worried' on Safety of Treasuries" (Update 2), Bloomberg.com, March 13, 2009. www.bloomberg.com/apps/news?pid=21070001&sid=aXW9GUdIySss (Accessed August 3, 2010).

3. Christie, Rebecca "Geithner to Reassure China U.S. Will Control Deficits" (Update 1), Bloomberg.com, May 31, 2009. www.bloomberg.com/apps/news?pid=21070001&sid=afg8MXnVGSGo (Accessed August 3, 2010).

4. Carey, Nick, "Foreign Ownership of U.S. Companies Jumps," Reuters, August 27, 2008. www.reuters.com/assets/print?aid=USN2744743020080827 (Accessed May 14, 2010).

5. Ibid.

6. Biesanz, Magdalene, "Foreign Investors, Water Supply Play into Rising Iowa Land Value," *Le Mars Daily Sentinel*, December 12, 2007. www.lemarsentinel.com/story/1297042.html (Accessed July 13, 2010).

7. Carvalho, Leticia, "Chinese Tourists Buying Foreclosure Properties," Real Estate Pro Articles, December 29, 2007. www.realestateproarticles.com via title search (Accessed September 25, 2010).

8. Miller, Leslie, "U.S. Toll Roads Increasingly Sold to Foreign Countries," Associated Press, July 16, 2006, and Steven Malanga, "The New Privatization," *City Journal*, Summer, 2007. www.city-journal.org/printable.php?id=2297 (Accessed September 26, 2010).

9. Blundell-Wignall, A., Hu, Y., and Yermo, J. "Sovereign Wealth and Pension Fund Issues," *OECD Working Papers on Insurance and Private Pensions*, 2008, No. 14, OECD Publishing. doi:10.1787/243287223503

10. Sovereign Wealth Fund Institute, "Sovereign Wealth Fund Rankings," (Updated June 2010.) www.swfinstitute.org via Fund Rankings tab (Accessed October 2, 2010).

11. Governance and Accountability Institute, Inc., "Information for You: The Growing Importance of Sovereign Wealth Funds (SWFs)," 2009. www.ga-institute.com/swf-matters/information-for-you-the-growing-importance-of-sovereign-wealth-funds.html (Accessed August 4, 2010).

12. Friedman, Thomas L., *The World Is Flat*, New York: Farrar, Straus and Giroux, 2005, p. 420.

13. Maslakovic, Marko, "Sovereign Wealth Funds 2008,"[Report] *IFSL Reasearch*, International Financial Services London, April 2008.

14. Cornwell, Rupert, "The Lobbyists' Scandal: The Secret World of Washington," *The Independent,* Independent Newspapers, Ltd., (UK), June 30,2005.

15. Arends, Brett, "What a Sovereign-Debt Crisis Could Mean for You," *The Wall Street Journal*, December 18, 2009.

16. Ibid.

Trend 3: Healthcare on Life Support

1.   Social Security and Medicare Boards of Trustees, *Status of the Social Security and Medicare Programs: A Summary of the 2009 Annual Reports,* Social Security Administration, www.ssa.gov/OACT/TRSUM/index.html. (Accessed January 13, 2010).

2.   Ibid.

3.   Davis, K., Schoen, C., Schoenbaum, S.C., Doty, M.M., Holmgren, A.L., Kriss, J.L., and Shea, K.K., "Mirror, Mirror on the Wall: An International Update on the Comparative Performance of American Healthcare," [Report] The Commonwealth Fund, May 15, 2007.

4.   Himmelstein, David U.,MD, Thorne, Deborah, PhD, Warren, Elizabeth Warren, JD, and Woolhandler, Steffie, MD, "Medical Bankruptcy in the United States, 2007: Results of a National Study," *The American Journal of Medicine*, Volume 122, Issue 8, August 2009. Note: A review by the author found criticism questioning whether the number of bankruptcies calculated in the study might be overstated, however the review did not find critics denying the problem exists.

5. "MEDICARE: Expensive, Successful/MEDICAID: Chaotic, Irre-vocable." *Time Magazine*, October 6, 1967. http://www.time.com/time/magazine/article/0,9171,844138,00.html (Accessed October 4, 2010).

6. Ibid.

7. Ginsburg, Paul B., "Can Hospitals and Physicians Shift the Effects of Cuts in Medicare Reimbursement to Private Payers?" October 8, 2003, Health Affairs, Project HOPE. http://content.healthaffairs.org/cgi/content/full/hlthaff.w3.472v1/DC1 (Accessed August 1, 2010).

8. Centers for Medicare and Medicaid Services, "Trustees Report & Trust Funds Overview," U.S. Department of Health and Human Services, August, 2010. http://www.cms.gov/ReportsTrustFunds/ (Accessed August 11, 2010).

9. Rutland Regional Medical Center, "Cost Shift." http://www.rrmc.org/upload/photos/175Cost_Shift.pdf (Accessed August 1,2010)

10. Mann, Cindy, Alker, Joan C., and Barish, David, "Medicaid and State Budgets: Looking at the Facts," Center for Children and Families, Georgetown University Health Policy Institute, May, 2008. http://ccf.georgetown.edu/index/cms-filesystem-action?file=ccf%20publications/about%20medicaid/nasbo%20final%205-1-08.pdf. Also, http://ccf.georgetown.edu via article title or date under Publications tab (Accessed October 3, 2010).

11. "Healthcare Costs are Hurting 57% of Fast-Growing Private Busi-nesses." *Trendsetter Barometer*, PricewaterhouseCoopers, November 14, 2007. http://www.barometersurveys.com/production/barsurv.nsf/vwallnewsbydocid/E2C0B143709FD120852573930051B8A4. Also www.barometersurveys.com via title search under Trendsetter Barometer tab (Accessed October 3, 2010).

12. Martin, Daniel, "A&E Patients Left in Ambulances for up to FIVE Hours So Trusts Can Meet Government Targets,'" Mail Online, February 18, 2008. http://www.dailymail.co.uk/news/article-515332/A-E-patients-left-ambulances-FIVE-hours-trusts-meet-government-tar-gets.html (Accessed October 4, 2010).

13. Forbes, Steve and Ames, Elizabeth, *How Capitalism Will Save Us: Why Free People and Free Markets Are the Best Answer in Today's Economy.* New York: Crown Business, November 2009.

14. Pardes, Herbert, "The Coming Shortage of Doctors," *The Wall Street Journal*, November 5, 2009, p.A19.

15. U.S. Preventive Services Task Force, Agency for Healthcare Re-search and Quality "Screening for Breast Cancer," release date:

November 2009, Updated: December, 2009. Http;//www.ahrq.gov/clinic/uspsbrca.htm. (Accessed August 4, 2010) and CNN, "U.S. Health Chief: No Change on Mammogram Policy," CNN.com, November 18, 2009. http;//www.cnn.com/2009/HEALTH/11/18/mammogram.guidelines/index.html (Accessed August 4, 2010).

16. Hand, Larry, "Employee Wellness Programs Prod Workers to Adopt Healthy Lifestyles," *Employer Health Incentives*, Harvard School of Public Health, Winter 2009, and CNN.com

17. "Better Employee Health on the Way," *Trend Letter*, Volume 27, Number 9, August 2008, p.12.

18. "Paying Employees to Lose pounds," *Trend Letter*, Volume 26, Number 7, June 2007, p. 6.

19. "Health Information Online," *Summary of Findings*, Pew Internet & American Life Project, Pew Research Center, May 17, 2005. http://www.pewinternet.org/Reports/2005/Health-Information-Online.aspx?r=1 (Accessed August 3, 2010).

20. "Study Finds Consumers Are Taking More Responsibility for Health-Care Decisions, and Physicians Face Increasing Competition," April 12, 2007. http://www.boozallen.com/news/33114276 (Accessed August 3, 2010).

21. Fox, Susannah, "Online Health Search 2006," [Report] Pew Internet and American Life Project, Pew Research Center , October 29, 2006. http://www.pewinternet.org/Reports/2006/Online-Health-Search-2006.aspx . (Accessed August 3, 2010).

22. "Here Comes the Healthcare Coach," *Trend Letter*, Volume 26, Number 4, March 2007, pp.1–2.

23. Rabin, Roni Caryn, "You Can Find Dr. Right, With Some Effort," *New York Times*, September 30, 2008. http://www.nytimes.com/2008/09/30/health/30find.html?_r=1&pagewanted=print (Accessed October 4, 2010).

24. Herrick, Devon, "Medical Tourism: Global Competition in Health Care," National Center for Policy Analysis, November 1, 2007. http://www.ncpa.org/pub/st304?pg=3 (Accessed January 16, 2010).

25. Francis, Walton, "Putting Medicare Consumers in Charge: Lessons from the FEHBP," American Enterprise Institute, October, 2009. http://www.aei.org/book/100022 (Accessed September 3, 2010).

Trend 4: China Stands Up

1. "China Ends U.S.'s Reign as Largest Auto Market (Update2)," Bloomberg.com., January 11, 2010. http://www.bloomberg.com/ apps/news?pid=newsarchive&sid=aE.x_r_19NZE. (Accessed July, 14, 2010).

2. Newcomb, Amelia, "Is China Japan All Over Again?" *The Christian Science Monitor*, August 19, 2005, pp.1–4.

3. Kate, Daniel Ten, "Free-Trade Agreement Between China, ASEAN Grouping Comes into Force," *The China Post*, January 1, 2010. http://www.chinapost.com.tw/print/238917.htm. (Accessed July 14, 2010).

4. Zissis, Carin, and Bajoria, Jayshree, "China's Environmental Crisis," Council on Foreign Relations, August 4, 2008. http://www.cfr. org/publication/12608/. (Accessed October 4, 2010).

5. Kwok, Vivian Wai-yin, "China Cracks Down for Product Safety," Forbes.com, August 24, 2007. http://www.forbes.com/2007/08/24/ china-quality-control-markets-equity-cx_vk_0824markets14.htmland. (Accessed January 16, 2010).

6. McKinsey and Company, "Addressing China's Looming Talent Shortage" *Perspective*, October, 2006. http://www.mckinsy.com/mgi/ publications/chinatalent.asp. (Accessed August 3, 2010).

7. Epstein, Gady, "Ponzi in Peking," *Forbes*, December 28, 2009, pp.72–74

8. Ibid.

9. Prasso, Sheridan, "American Made...Chinese Owned," *Fortune* magazine, May 24, 2010, pp.84-92.

10. Ibid.

11. Dorn, James A., "China Grows Faster, Higher, Stronger," *Far Eastern Economic Review*, August 11, 2008.

12. Karabell, Zachary, "Deficits and the Chinese Challenge," *The Wall Street Journal*, October 13, 2009, p.A19. Also: Zachary Karabell, *Superfusion: How China and America Became One Economy and Why the World's Prosperity Depends On It*, New York: Simon & Schuster, October 2009.

13. Russell, Richard, "Richard's Remarks," *Dow Theory Letters*, July 12, 2010, p.1. http://www.dowtheoryletters.com. (Accessed July 12, 2010).

Trend 5: The Employed, the Under-Employed, and the Unemployable

1. Reich, Robert, "The Jobs Picture Still Looks Bleak," *The Wall Street Journal*, April 12, 2010, p.A19.
2. Sum, Andrew and Khatiwada, Ishwar, "Labor Utilization Problems of U.S. Workers Across Household Income Groups at the End of the Great Recession," Center for Labor Market Studies, Northeastern University, February 2010.
3. Gordon, Edward, "Current Recession Masks Imminent Talent Gap," *Trend Letter*, June 2009, p. 3.
4. Manpower, Inc., "2010 Talent Shortage Survey Results," May 2010, pp.3–5, 14.
5. "10 Trends that Will Change the Way You Do Business," *The Kiplinger Letter*, January, 2009, p.5.
6. Alliance for Excellent Education, "The High Cost of High School Dropouts," *Issue Brief*, August, 2009. http://www.all4ed.org/files/high cost.pdf. (Accessed August 14, 2010).
7. Ibid.
8. EPE Research Center, "Cities in Crisis: Closing the Education Gap," [Report], Editorial Projects in Education, Inc., April, 2009.
9. Glasmeier, Amy and Salant, Priscilla, "Low Skill Workers in Rural America Face Permanent Job Loss," *Policy Brief*, No. 2, The Carsey Institute, Spring 2006. http://www.carseyinstitute.unh.edu/publications/PB_displacedworkers_06.pdf. (Accessed January 17, 2010).

Trend 6: America's Spending Binge

1. Coggan, Philip, "Repent at Leisure," *The Economist*, June 26, 2010, p. 4. Article includes quote from Roland Nash, Chief Strategist at Renaissance Capital.
2. Carlini, James, "Fixing Digital Infrastructure," Carlini's Comments, September 4, 2009. http://carliniscomments.com/archives/2009/09/summary.html (Accessed July 17, 2010).
3. deMause, Neil, "Stealth IRS Changes Mean Millions of New Tax Forms," CNNMoney.com, May 21, 2010. http://money.cnn.com/2010/05/21/smallbusiness/1099_deluge/index.htm. (Accessed July 31, 2010).
4. "KABC, "Late Push for Governor's Ballot Props," ABClocal.go.com, May 20, 2009. http://abclocal.go.com/kabc/story?section=news/politics/local_elections&id=6820444 (Accessed July 31, 2010).

5. "Millionaires Go Missing," *The Wall Street Journal*, May 26, 2009, p.A18. The conclusions therein were challenged by *The Economist*, in the "Case of the missing millionaires," June 1, 2010. http://www. economist.com. and Google article by title (Accessed August 2, 2010).

6. Pew Center on the States, "The Trillion Dollar Gap," February 2010, pp.3–5.

7. Ibid.

8. Aden, Mary Anne and Aden, Pamela, "Financial Crises of the Past," *The Chartist Mutual Fund Letter*, March 5, 2009, p.4. From "Selected Quotes" included in the *Chartist Mutual Fund Letter*.

Trend 7: Prices Gone Wild

1. Bernanke, Ben, "Deflation: Making Sure It Doesn't Happen Here," Remarks by Governor Ben S. Bernanke before the National Economists Club, Washington D.C., [Speech],The Federal Reserve Board, November 21, 2010

2. "Historical CPI," InflationData.com, http://inflationdata.com/inflation/Consumer_Price_Index/ (Accessed November 24, 2009).

3. Ibid.

4. Gordon, John Steele, "The Man Who Wasn't There," *American Heritage Magazine*, November 1991, pp.20-22.

5. Oxford English Dictionary, Eleventh edition, Oxford: Oxford University Press, 2004.

6. Ibid.

7. Wolfram, Gary, PhD, "Econ 101: Spike in Money Supply Caused Inflation," [Commentary], Business & Media Institute, August 27, 2008. http://www.businessandmedia.org/commentary/2008/20080827135845.aspx. (Accessed August 2, 2010).

8. "What is Deflation?" InflationData.com, http://inflationdata.com/inflation/Inflation_Articles/Deflation.asp. (Accessed July 10, 2010).

9. Shargal, Meir and Houseman Capgemini, Doug, "Myths and Realties of Renewable Energy," SmartGridNews.com, April 3, 2009. www.smartgridnews.com/artman/publish/commentary. Also: www.smartgridnews.com (Accessed August 2, 2010).

10. Berman, Saul J., Christner, Richard, and Bell, Ragna, "After The Crisis: What Now?" [Executive Report], IBM Global Business Services, March 2010, pp.2–3, 10.

11. Paul, Katie Paul, "Dying on the Vine," *Newsweek,* August 24, 2009. www.newsweek.com/id/211381. (Accessed December 9, 2009).

Trend 8: The Demographic Time Bomb

1. U.S. Census Bureau, "Oldest Baby Boomers Turn 60!" January 3, 2006. www.census.gov. http://www.census.gov/PressRelease/www/releases/archives/facts_for_features_special_editions/006105.html. (Accessed July 14, 2010).
2. Ibid.
3. Greenspan, Alan, "Remarks by Chairman Alan Greenspan to the Federal Reserve Bank of Philadelphia Forum, Philadelphia, Pennsylvania," The Federal Reserve Board, December 2, 2005.
4. Walker, David M., "Addressing Fiscal Sustainability and Fixing the Social Security System," United States Government Accountability Office (GAO), February 14, 2008, GAO-08-524CG.
5. Institute of Medicine of the National Academies, "Retooling for an Aging America: Building the Healthcare Workforce," [Report Brief], April 2008.
6. U.S.Bureau of Labor Statistics, "Consumer Expenditures Survey 2004," Table 3. http://www.bls.gov/cex/2004/Standard/age.pdf (Accessed October 4, 2010).
7. Congressional Budget Office, "The Retirement Prospects of the Baby Boomers," Economic and Budget Issue Brief, March 18, 2004.
8. Rosenberg, Yuval, "The Boomer Bust," *Fortune,* June 19, 2006.
9. Molony, Walter, "Baby Boomer Study Shows Changing Housing Needs, Uncertain Retirement," Realtor.org, October 16, 2006. http://www.realtor.org/press_room/news_releases/2006/10/baby_boomer_study_06. Also: via title search. (Accessed January 27, 2010).

Trend 9: The Knock Heard 'Round The World

1. Carlini, James, "Will We Butt up Against the Web's Limitations?," Carlini's Comments, April 24,2008. http://www.carliniscomments.com/archives/2008/04/summary.html. (Accessed July 17, 2010).
2. Bayne, Jay S., PhD, Echelon, LLC, [Commentary at technology forum, Milwaukee, Wisconsin], June 4, 2003. Quote was qualified by author in a follow up telephone conversation with Dr. Bayne.
3. "Countries of the World (populations)," WorldAtlas.com, February 2006. http://www.worldatlas.com/atlas/populations/ctypopls.htm (Accessed August 16, 2010).

4. Bellman, Eric, "Indian Firms Shift Focus to the Poor," *The Wall Street Journal*, October 21, 2009, p.1.

5. Congressional Budget Office, "An Economic Analysis of the Revenue Provisions of OBRA–93," January 1994.

6. Foreign Affairs and International Trade Canada, "Fast Facts: North American Trade Agreement," Date modified: December 15, 2009. http://www.international.gc.ca. (Accessed August 2, 2010).

7. "English still language of business," *Phoenix Business Journal*, September 5, 2008. http://phoenix.bizjournals.com/phoenix/stories/2008/09/08/smallb2.html. (Accessed August 14, 2010).

8. Ibid.

9. Chanda, Nayan, "Wake Up and Face the Flat Earth," [Interview], Thomas L. Friedman, author, *The World is Flat*, for Global Vision, published by Yale Global, September 22, 2005. http://www.globalenvision.org/library/2/803. (Accessed July 17, 2010).

10. Hilton, Anthony, "Turmoil Tests the New World Order," ThisIsMoney.co.uk, January 24, 2008. http://www.thisismoney.co.uk/news/columnists/article.html?in_article_id=429689&in_page_id=19&in_author_id=4. (Accessed August 14, 2010).

11. "America Leaves Itself Behind," *The Wall Street Journal*, November 11, 2009, p.A20.

12. Evenett, Simon J., ED, "Broken Promises: A G-20 Summit Report by Global Trade Alert," Centre for Economic Policy Research, September 17, 2009.

13. Menon, Nirmala, "Canada Asks WTO to Settle U.S. Spat," *The Wall Street Journal*, October 8, 2009, p.A9.

14. Johnson, Ian, "China Strikes Back on Trade," *The Wall Street Journal*, September 14, 2009, p.A1.

15. Kanter, James, "At Climate Talks, Trade Pressures Mount," *New York Times*, December 17, 2009. http://www.nytimes.com/2009/12/18/science/earth/18trade.html?_r=2. (Accessed August 2, 2010).

16. "The Black Liquor War," *The Wall Street Journal*, June 29, 2009, A12. Provides the American point of view on this trade dispute. For the Canadian perspective, see: "Federal Government Rolls Out $1 B Aid Plan for Pulp and Paper Producers," *CBC News*, June 17, 2009. http://www.cbc.ca/money/story/2009/06/17/raitt-pulp-assistance.html. (Accessed December 3, 2009).

17. "Mexico Retaliates," *The Wall Street Journal*, March 19, 2009, p.A14.

Trend 10: Talent Matters

1. "The Search for Talent," *The Economist*, October 7, 2006, p.11.
2. Di Romualdo, Tony, "The Misguided Talent War," *Wisconsin Technology Network*, November 09, 2006. http://wistechnology.com/articles/3471/. (Accessed January 24, 2010).
3. Tam, Pui-Wang, "CIO Jobs Morph from Tech Support into Strategy," *The Wall Street Journal*, February 20, 2007, p.B1.
4. "Demographics," *Ag 101*, U.S. Environmental Protection Agency, September 10, 2009. http://www.epa.gov/oecaagct/ag101/demographics.html. (Accessed July 28, 2010).
5. Ward, William A, "Manufacturing Productivity and the Shifting U.S., China and Global Job Scene—1990 to 2005," *CIT Working Paper*, 052507, Clemson University Center for International Trade, August 4, 2005.
6. Gordon, Edward, "Current Recession Masks Imminent Talent Gap," *Trend Letter*, June, 2009, p.3.
7. Manpower Inc., "10 for 2010," *n.d.*

Your Plan B: Winning Strategies

1. Gladwell, Malcolm, *The Tipping Point*, Boston: Back Bay Books, 2000, pp.15–29.

Index

About the Author

L.A. Jenkins uses his extensive business experience, education, and wide network of sources in his studies of cycles, trends, and situation analyses to provide practical guidance through uncertain times.

After creating an international company based on game-changing innovation, Jenkins, as CEO, navigated the company successfully through the economic meltdown of 2008–09. During 2008, Jenkins moved most of his investment portfolios to largely cash positions prior to the subsequent stock market meltdown in the fall of that year. The key to these successes was Jenkins's ability to effectively forecast business developments and adapt new business and investment models to take advantage of those developments.

Jenkins is an experienced inventor, investor, speaker, author, business coach, and university instructor, and serves on the Board of Directors for non-profit and for-profit organizations. He is a Certified Internet Business Strategist, a U.S. patent recipient, and holds an MBA.

For more information and up-to-date predictions,
visit the author's website: www.jenkinsusa.com